# The
# Great 5-Ingredient
## COOKBOOK

# The Great 5-Ingredient COOKBOOK

## 250 Simple, Healthy Dishes in Less Than 30 Minutes

Reader's Digest

The Reader's Digest Association, Inc.
New York, NY | Montreal

# contents

Time today is precious.
And so are family and friends.

Sometimes it can be hard to find the time for simple pleasures such as cooking and sharing meals with loved ones. Today it is so easy to resort to buying junk food or prepackaged meals on your way home at the end of a busy day, too tired or simply too uninspired to cook a meal.

But cooking really needn't be a chore. This inspiring book shows how good food with minimal cooking and preparation really is achievable, at home, every day. Our magic formula — 5 ingredients and only 10 minutes preparation and 15 minutes cooking — adds up to dinner on the table in under 30 minutes.

You'll be astonished how many great meals you can prepare with a minimum of ingredients and minimum of fuss — from brunch and breakfast to soups, salads, starters, snacks and hearty mains, right through to delicious desserts.

Our cooking experts have scoured the world's greatest cuisines to bring you delicious everyday family meals, as well as quick, modern versions of traditional classics, and fabulous dishes you can make in a snap for special meals with friends. Beautifully photographed, our simple recipes emphasise fresh, easy-to-find produce, but also make the most of healthy convenience foods and shortcut ingredients.

This book is also packed with tricks of the trade — time-saving cooking tips, recipe variations and finishing touches to glam up simple meals. Each chapter has a special feature packed with brilliantly versatile recipe ideas, and our chapter on 'Basics' at the back of the book provides quick recipes for handy sauces, pastes and spice mixtures to instantly jazz up a host of dishes.

Minimising your shopping list will help cut your thinking time and also your shopping time. And by having to buy fewer ingredients, spending less on takeaways or food-to-go and no more wasted food in the fridge, you'll soon start counting up the savings!

We hope this book helps you slash your hours in the kitchen and dish up meals with flair. Here's to many memorable, pleasurable, stress-free meals to come.

*The Editors*

# Welcome to fast, fabulous cooking

The perennial question 'What's for dinner?' has vexed many of us at some point. Unfortunately, in the busy lives we lead today, something has to give — and often it is dinner. At the end of the working day, if there's nothing at home ready to serve up quickly, fast food becomes the easy option, and everyone suffers in the long run. We are here to help!

## How our recipes work

This book offers a great collection of recipes designed to be made quickly and easily.

- Each recipe has no more than **5 ingredients**.
- Each recipe has a preparation time of no more than **10 minutes**.
- Each recipe has a cooking time of no more than **15 minutes**.

For practical reasons, we aren't including salt, pepper, oil or water in our '5 ingredients' count.

As well as being quick and convenient, each recipe also has handy tips and hints, with variations where appropriate so you can substitute other ingredients or otherwise adapt the recipes as desired. Serving suggestions are also given where suitable, but feel free to serve the dishes with as much or as little in the way of accompaniments as you like.

Whether you're hankering for a soup, quick snack or simple starter, or tasty ideas for chicken, seafood, meat, pasta and vegetables, followed by a lusciously quick dessert, we'll have you fabulously well fed with a minimum of fuss. As well as great weeknight meals for any season, you'll also find many dishes you'll be happy to serve to dinner guests.

On the following pages you'll find simple tips on stocking your pantry and organising your kitchen for maximum efficiency. Our Basics chapter at the end of the book also provides quick recipes for versatile sauces, pastes and spice mixtures and sweet treats that are great to have on hand.

## The secret ingredient: planning ahead

This may sound a little over-zealous, but the absolute key to quick meals is planning. A little time spent on the weekend working out even a rough meal plan for the week will pay off handsomely, because you'll know exactly what ingredients you'll need to have on hand. Having a simple shopping list will then save you a lot of time and money at the supermarket, and helps ensure everything doesn't fall in a heap at dinnertime. You'll also be eating more healthily than if you were relying on takeaway (takeout) meals.

Go through the pantry to see what you have and what you will need. You may like to stock up on non-perishables, and pick up the fresh produce every couple of days if that works for you. The fewer trips to the shops the better though, as inevitably you will be tempted into some impulse purchase.

When you have a little spare time, also think about creating your own 'fast foods' by cooking up a double batch of soups, bakes or slow-cooked stews. Portion, package and label the extras, then pop them into the freezer so you can enjoy quick home-cooked meals during the week. These will be greatly appreciated, especially in the colder months.

You can whip up lots of fresh, tasty meals with just 5 quality ingredients, plus a splash of olive oil, salt and pepper.

## Keeping it real

Supermarkets are bursting with pre-made meals, pre-cooked foods, jars of sauces, packets of flavour mixtures and meal 'bases' and 'kits'. The challenge is to use these to your advantage without falling into the processed food trap.

Take a little time to read labels and consider if there is a healthier option — basically, try to choose foods that are as close to their natural state as possible. If you do feel the need to use some of the more processed convenience products, just use a bit of commonsense to help you achieve a healthy balance over the week.

## Time vs money

Pre-prepared foods, such as packaged grated cheese as opposed to cheese in a block, can be a little more expensive. When choosing which type to buy, weigh up the advantages of the time saved — also taking into account the cleaning up — and decide where your priorities lie. For people who are time-poor or hate fussing around, the time saved can be worth the money.

## Tricks to save time and trouble

- Do a weekly meal plan and write a shopping list.
- Don't shop when you're tired or hungry, as you'll be more easily distracted.
- Grab extras of products you use often — especially if they're on sale.
- Make it fun: find a local farmers market for super-fresh produce, and get the family involved.
- Buy in-season produce — it will be cheaper, tastier and more nutritious.

# Just ⑤ ingredients…

Having a well-stocked pantry, fridge and freezer is the best insurance against dinnertime dramas. Your pantry, fridge and freezer don't have to be large, just well organised and neatly kept so you can find things easily. Store any opened packets of dry goods in airtight containers to keep them fresh and tidy, and use up the older ingredients first.

## In the pantry

Ideally the pantry should be a cool dark place, where the food is stored out of direct light.

### Packets

Dry ingredients should be transferred to airtight containers once opened.

● **Rice** cooks quickly, but if you want to prepare rice even more quickly, a number of par-cooked (par-boiled) and pre-cooked products are available.

● **Pasta** is such a great staple, and can be easily transformed into a meal with the addition of a few other ingredients.

● **Asian-style noodles** are widely available these days, and are usually very quick to prepare and cook. Look for fresh noodles in vacuum-sealed pouches, or dried noodles — they both have a long shelf life and are handy for a quick stir-fry or soup.

● **Instant couscous** is the quickest of all starches to prepare, and actually needs no cooking at all, just soaking in boiling water. You can add some stock or juice for extra flavour, or use the couscous as a plain base to soak up sauces.

### Cans

Some canned foods are especially indispensable in a well-stocked pantry. Canned goods should ideally be used within 12 months of purchase, though they will often keep much longer if the cans are not rusted or dented (which can affect the seal). Unused contents should be transferred to airtight containers and refrigerated; they will keep for up to 3 days.

● **Tomatoes** are invaluable for whipping up a quick pasta sauce, pizza topping or adding body and flavour to soups and stews.

● **Tuna, salmon and sardines** are a quick protein base for pasta dishes and salads.

● **Pulses such as beans, chickpeas and lentils** are time-consuming to cook from scratch, but the canned varieties are perfectly acceptable and simply need to be heated through. They can also be served at room temperature in salads, or puréed to make a dip or accompaniment to meat.

● **Coconut milk** gives a delicious, authentic depth of flavour and creamy texture to curries and soups.

● **Canned fruit**, especially varieties with a short growing season, make for speedy, delicious desserts. Peaches, pears, apricots and plums are great.

### Jars & bottles

Products in glass bottles should keep for about 2 years, although the label instructions often recommend storing them in the fridge once opened. Products in plastic bottles have a shorter shelf life and should carry a 'use-by' or 'best before' date.

● **Oil** starts and/or finishes many recipes — from sautéeing onion and garlic, to dressing and drizzling over meals. A basic olive oil and vegetable oil will do for cooking, though you may like to use peanut oil for stir-frying, and have a good extra virgin olive oil for dressing salads and vegetables.

● **Spray oil** makes quick work of any jobs where you once would have used a brush to apply the oil, such as greasing pans.

● **Vinegar** can be used to make a simple salad dressing with olive oil, or to deglaze a pan after frying meat. A white wine vinegar, red wine vinegar and balsamic vinegar are a good basic start, then you can look at flavoured vinegars such as tarragon vinegar. Herbed vinegars are great if you want to add flavour without chopping.

### Versatile shortcut ingredients

- Pasta & dried noodles
- Couscous
- Canned tomatoes
- Canned salmon & tuna
- Liquid stock, or stock (bouillon) cubes or powder
- Canned beans, chickpeas & lentils
- Cheese and eggs
- Jars of chopped ginger, garlic & chilli

- **Sauces** are myriad; many can be used in cooking as well as a condiment on cooked food. Asian sauces such as soy and teriyaki can be added during cooking, or used as a marinade base. Chilli sauce will give even a simple omelette a bit of oomph, while tomato sauce (ketchup) is essential for a barbecue. Pasta sauces can be used not only on pasta, but on pizzas, in pies and bakes and as a soup base.

- **Pastes such as Indian or Thai curry pastes** take the time and work out of the labour-intensive process of making the paste from scratch, and are a delicious base for a quick meal. Tomato paste (concentrated purée) adds depth of flavour and colour to soups, stews and sauces.

- **Chopped ginger, chilli and garlic** in jars are super time savers! Store them in the fridge once opened.

## In the fridge

As well as fresh vegetables, keep these versatile basics. Store the oldest items at the front for easy retrieval and to avoid accidental wastage.

- **Eggs** for an omelette or frittata, or simply boiled and served with toast soldiers — you can't go past eggs for a tasty nutritious 'convenience' food.

- **Cheese** comes in many shapes and forms, but a basic block of cheddar and a good parmesan will help out in many dinnertime dilemmas. A tangy blue, creamy brie or camembert and a salty fetta are other favourites that can be added to many dishes for a luxurious taste and texture.

- **Milk, cream and butter** enrich sauces and soups. A knob of butter on anything improves it instantly!

## In the freezer

These incredibly handy ingredients have saved many a desperate cook.

**Frozen pastry** — whether shortcrust, puff or filo — take the time and bother out of making pies and tarts. Look for ready-rolled sheets of pastry, which thaw quickly.

**Peas** from the freezer are often tastier than fresh peas, as they are frozen very quickly after harvest.

**Spinach** is great for soups or pies. It can be thawed in the microwave — just remember to squeeze out the excess liquid before using it.

**Berries** have such a short season, so having them in the freezer all year round is a treat. They don't hold their shape well once thawed, so use them in dishes (such as muffins or coulis) where their appearance isn't important.

**Meat** freezes well as long as it is packaged up correctly. Make sure it is airtight, label it and make sure you use it up within a reasonable time.

Stock your pantry with spices, condiments and canned, dried and bottled goods and you'll never be short of meal ideas.

# Just 10 minutes preparation...

Ten-minute preparation time is possible, but having the right equipment within easy reach will speed things up immensely. Think about which kitchen tools and appliances you use regularly, and how they can be stored for easy access. Without completely redesigning your kitchen, a quick assessment of what is working and what isn't can make a huge difference.

## Quick preparation tools

### Chopping

The most basic and essential kitchen tool for any cook is a decent knife. A large, good-quality chef's knife with a 20 cm (8 inch) blade and a sturdy handle makes any task a breeze, from cutting up hard vegetables to carving meat or finely chopping herbs. Together with a small paring knife and a serrated bread knife, these should be all you need. Get the best you can afford, learn how to keep a good edge with a steel, have them professionally sharpened occasionally, and store them properly.

Also keep a couple of chopping boards — either wooden or plastic — in different sizes. Scrub them well after use and allow them to air dry.

### Grating

You'll need a standard box grater with large and small holes for grating cheese, vegetables and other ingredients. A microplane is handy to finely grate ingredients such as chocolate or cheese directly onto a range of dishes.

### Crushing garlic

A garlic crusher is a great gadget for mincing garlic quickly. Place the peeled garlic clove into a garlic crusher and crush the garlic straight into the pan. For easy cleaning up, soak the crusher in a little water straight away, until it's time to wash up.

To peel garlic quickly, place it on a steady board and lay a wide-bladed knife on its side over the clove. Hit the knife sharply with the heel of your hand to flatten the garlic and to break the skin; it will then be very simple to remove.

### Draining

Use a fine mesh sieve to drain canned beans, vegetables or cooked rice, and a colander for draining cooked pasta and larger pieces of food. Rinse a used mesh sieve immediately after use, then tap it sharply on the edge of the sink to dislodge any food particles.

### Stirring

You can have metal spoons for folding, and wooden spoons for stirring (especially in non-stick pans) — or you can buy heatproof silicon spatulas, which will do both jobs. Store them in a convenient drawer, or standing upright in a jar close to your preparation area.

# Time-saving appliances

There are so many different kitchen labour-saving machines now available — a stroll through any electrical store will dazzle you with 'must-have' gadgets and gizmos. Depending on the dishes you like to prepare, you can assemble an arsenal of equipment, or stick to a few basics such as these, which will see you through most recipes.

## Food processor

A basic food processor has a large detachable bowl that sits on top of a sturdy motor base, and has a selection of blades. In it you can chop, grind, purée, make pastry or blend ingredients. These are very versatile, though they can be a little bulky.

## Blender

A blender purées food in an instant, though it does tend to make it frothy. It is probably best used for making drinks such as milkshakes and fruit smoothies.

## Hand-held stick blender

This gadget is plugged into power, but you can immerse it directly into a pot of soup to blend it to a smooth purée — very handy, as it saves having to transfer the soup to a food processor or blender, and also means much less washing up. New models also have a base-bowl that they can sit on to chop and grind, though these are usually quite small.

## Electric beaters

Either hand-held, or a free-standing machine with the bowl on a rotating base, these make quick work of creaming butter and sugar for cakes, as well as whipping cream or eggwhites.

# Savvy storage

Having time-saving equipment in the kitchen is only useful if you can easily access it. Appliances stored way out of sight, or which are tricky to get to, will never be used!

Look at any commercial kitchen and you will see that accessibility to equipment is paramount. Chopping boards, bowls, strainers and the like are stored on open shelving; pots, pans and implements hang from easily reachable hooks, and knives are stored in blocks or on magnetised strips on the wall. The point of all this is that you can reach out and grab whatever you need quickly.

Of course the home kitchen is quite a different place, but some of these storage ideas can be adapted easily, depending on your personal aesthetics and individual cooking style.

If you are planning a new kitchen, try not to be too distracted by fancy finishes, because practicality and efficiency are what will count in the long run.

## Handy tools for speedy preparation

- Chef's knife
- Hand-held stick blender
- Silicon spatulas
- Garlic crusher
- Microplane

A few well-chosen kitchen tools can cut preparation time and free your benches and cupboards of unnecessary clutter.

# Just (15) minutes cooking...

Once the food preparation is done, there's still the cooking, plating and finishing touches before dinner is on the table. While food can't always be hurried along — there's no point cooking over high heat if food ends up black on the outside and uncooked in the middle — here are some easy tips to get from raw ingredients to finished product as efficiently as possible.

## Time-saving cooking tips

Here are some ways to get things happening in the kitchen more quickly.

• To preheat the oven quickly, use the fan-forced setting if you have it. (Don't forget to then set it back to non fan-forced, if that is what you'll be baking or roasting with.)

• Preheat pans while you chop — though do keep an eye on them.

• While non-stick cookware doesn't actually make your food cook faster, it will save you time washing up as there won't be burnt bits stuck on it!

• To boil water quickly, use an electric kettle to do the job, then transfer the hot water to a pot. This is much quicker than bringing water to a boil in a pot. If you don't have an electric kettle, cover the pot tightly with a lid. After adding foods to boiling liquid, the temperature will drop, so cover the pot again to return the liquid to the boil.

• Think about timing. If you are cooking multiple elements of a recipe, consider which processes can be happening simultaneously.

## Time savers

Two cooking appliances worth investigating are the slow cooker and the pressure cooker.

While a slow cooker obviously isn't fast, you can simply pop in all your ingredients in the morning and let it cook away all day, coming home to a meal that is immediately ready to eat.

A pressure cooker on the other hand cooks food very quickly, and is particularly good for stews and casseroles, which usually have a long cooking time.

## Microwave know-how

A microwave oven is a standard item in most kitchens these days. It's a very useful appliance for the time-poor cook, especially for thawing cooked or raw foods, and reheating cooked food. Before using one it is best to familiarise yourself with the manufacturer's instructions as microwaves vary in wattage (strength), which determines the length of time it takes to thaw or cook food.

### Thawing

The microwave is an excellent tool for thawing frozen food, whether raw (such as meat or chicken), or cooked dishes like soups or stews. Remove the food from its packaging and place it on a microwave-safe plate. Check and turn the food often as it thaws, to ensure it does so evenly. To prevent spoilage, it is best to cook the food immediately after thawing, as the food may start to cook through in bits even as it is thawing.

Cooked dishes such as stews and curries can usually go straight from the freezer to the microwave to be thawed, then heated. Make sure the container is microwave-safe, or transfer the frozen food to an appropriate dish. As the food begins to thaw, stir it often to heat it through evenly.

### Cooking

Not all foods are suitable to cook in the microwave, but some certainly are. Vegetables are cooked in minimal water and so retain their colour and nutrients — particularly vegetables such as broccoli, green beans, carrots, pumpkin (winter squash) and peas. Remember to cut foods into even-sized pieces so they cook through at the same rate.

## Finishing touches

While time is of the essence when putting a meal together quickly, a simple finishing touch can transform a mundane dish into something special.

- A drizzle of extra virgin olive oil over a plated meal adds flair and extra flavour.

- Snip an appropriate herb over the final meal — if there are herbs in the dish, reserve a small quantity to finish the dish off.

- Depending on the type of dish you are preparing, you can serve food up on large platters for people to help themselves at the table, rather than worrying about plating up individually.

- Rather than making a dressing, put olive oil and balsamic vinegar on the table as condiments.

- Antipasto ingredients can look classy decanted from their plastic tubs or wrappings and piled onto a large white platter, with some crusty bread on the side.

- A baguette from the freezer can be thawed at room temperature, then refreshed by briefly splashing it under cold running water, then popped in the oven to crisp up while dinner cooks.

- Keep a box of canapé cups in the pantry for unexpected visitors. Add a dollop of pesto, or any kind of dip, and half a cherry tomato for instant party food.

- Don't underestimate the sandwich. Mix chopped cooked chicken with chopped herbs and a dollop of good-quality mayonnaise. Spread onto sliced bread, cut off the crusts, then cut into fingers and serve with champagne!

- Jazz up a bought frozen cheesecake by topping it with fresh seasonal fruit.

- Scoop icing (confectioners') sugar into a small sieve and dust it over a dessert or pudding.

- Add glamour to a chocolate dessert by adding a dusting of dark cocoa powder.

## Magic microwave tricks

- **To cook rice**, combine 1 cup rice with 1½ cups (375 ml) water in a microwave-safe bowl. Cover with plastic wrap and microwave for 12 minutes. This saves time bringing water to the boil in a saucepan.

- **Cook some pappadums** in the microwave, while your curry heats up in a pot, saving yourself an oily pan to clean up.

- **Make some popcorn** for a quick and healthy snack. Simply place ¼ cup (60 g) popping corn in a microwave-safe bowl, cover with plastic wrap and microwave for 2–3 minutes.

- **Make croutons** by brushing bread with a little olive oil. Cut the bread into cubes and arrange on a plate. Microwave in 1-minute bursts until crisp.

- **For the quickest-ever jacket (baked) potatoes**, scrub some potatoes well and prick with a fork. Rub them with olive oil and sprinkle with salt. Wrap in paper towels and microwave for 10–15 minutes, depending on their size, turning once halfway through cooking.

For consistent results, cut all your ingredients to a uniform size so they cook through evenly and at the same rate.

soups

# Soup it up!

Think outside the square when it comes to serving your favourite soup — a few little extra touches can transform a simple meal into something quite special.

## A luscious, creamy dollop

A spoonful of sour cream, mascarpone, crème fraîche or thick Greek-style yogurt dolloped onto a bowl of soup just before serving adds to its visual appeal as well as its flavour. These dollops also add a velvety texture when stirred into smooth, puréed soups, and can tone down the heat in many spicy soups. A sprinkle of chopped herbs on top of the dollop also looks great and adds fresh flavour.

## Brilliant flavour boosters

A simple soup will benefit from a final swirl of one of these flavour-packed extras.

### Gremolata

This simple combination of chopped fresh parsley, finely grated lemon zest and finely chopped or crushed garlic is delicious on seafood or tomato-based soups.

### Harissa

Just a small spoonful of this spicy North African paste packs quite a punch — so add a little at first, and then more if needed. Harissa is available in tubes or small jars from some delicatessens, or you can easily make your own (see Basics, page 310).

### Pesto

This Italian basil paste adds depth to minestrone and other tomato-based soups. Use the recipe on page 310 to make your own, or buy some in jars from the supermarket.

### Sun-dried tomato pesto

This variation on traditional pesto adds a rich tomato flavour. In a food processor, blend some chopped sun-dried tomatoes, grated parmesan, toasted pine nuts and extra virgin olive oil to a smooth paste. The pesto will keep in the fridge for up to 1 week.

# Crunch time

Add an element of texture with a crunchy soup topping, or crispy bread morsels served on the side.

## Sippets

Cut the crusts from day-old bread, then cut the bread into cubes. Heat about 2 cm (¾ inch) olive oil in a small frying pan and fry the bread until crisp and golden brown. Drain on paper towels and sprinkle lightly with salt. Scatter over your soup at serving time.

## Baked croutons

Preheat the oven to 190°C (375°F/Gas 5). Cut a garlic clove in half and infuse it in some extra virgin olive oil for about 15 minutes. Remove the crusts from day-old bread (firmly textured Italian-style or sourdough bread is especially good), then tear or cut the bread into small pieces. Drizzle with the garlic oil and toss to coat. Spread on a baking tray and bake until crisp and golden.

## Turkish soldiers

Cut pide (Turkish flat bread) into thin slices. Toast under a hot grill (broiler) until golden brown on both sides. Drizzle with extra virgin olive oil and serve.

## Cheesy crostini

Cut a baguette into 1 cm (½ inch) slices and toast under a hot grill (broiler) until golden. Sprinkle with grated cheese, then grill (broil) until melted and bubbling. Serve hot.

## Parmesan crisps

Preheat the oven to 190°C (375°F/Gas 5) and line a baking tray with baking (parchment) paper. Spread level tablespoons of finely grated parmesan into 7 cm (2¾ inch) rounds on the baking tray. Bake for 3–4 minutes, or until the cheese is bubbling and lightly golden at the edges. Leave on the tray for about 1 minute, then lift onto a wire rack to cool completely. Serve with soup.

## Bread roll bowls

Instead of serving your soup with bread, try serving it in bread! This type of presentation suits a thick, puréed soup. Preheat the oven to 180°C (350°F/Gas 4). Cut the tops from large crusty bread rolls, then pull out the bread inside, leaving a 'wall' about 1.5 cm (⅝ inch) thick. Place the hollow rolls on a baking tray, along with the lids, and bake for 5 minutes, or until warm and crisp. Place on shallow plates and ladle the soup into them. Serve immediately.

## Pie-top soup

Preheat the oven to 200°C (400°F/Gas 6). Ladle warm soup into small deep ovenproof bowls or ramekins. Cut out rounds of puff pastry a little larger than the bowl tops. Cover the bowls with the pastry, pressing the pastry onto the rims of the bowls, then set them on a large baking tray. Brush the tops with lightly beaten egg and sprinkle with sesame or poppy seeds if desired. Bake for 15–20 minutes, or until the tops are puffed and golden brown.

# Chicken noodle soup

This comforting soup is very versatile. Experiment with different types of noodles, or use broken-up angel hair pasta. Try adding Asian vegetables and flavours and serving with lime wedges.

**6 cups (1.5 litres) chicken stock**
**½ teaspoon Chinese five-spice**
**2 boneless, skinless chicken breasts, about 200 g (7 oz) each**
**100 g (3½ oz) rice vermicelli noodles**
**⅔ cup (30 g) fresh coriander (cilantro) leaves**

1  Fill an electric kettle with water and bring to a boil. Place the stock and five-spice in a large saucepan; cover and bring to a boil.

2  Meanwhile, thinly slice the chicken. Add the chicken to the hot stock, then cover and keep at a simmer for 5–10 minutes, or until the chicken is cooked.

3  Place the noodles in a heatproof bowl, pour the boiling water over and soak for 2 minutes, or until softened. Drain the noodles, then cut into shorter lengths using scissors.

4  Stir the noodles and half the coriander through the soup. Ladle into serving bowls, sprinkle with the remaining coriander and serve.

**Serving suggestion**
Serve with lime wedges for squeezing over, and some chopped fresh chilli if desired.

## Variations
- Add some thinly julienned carrot, celery, fresh ginger, corn kernels and/or sliced spring onions (scallions).
- Instead of fresh chicken, buy a barbecued chicken, shred the meat and simmer it in step 2 until heated through.

PREPARATION 10 minutes

COOKING 15 minutes

SERVES 4

## Quick tip
Using an electric kettle to boil the water for the noodles speeds up the preparation time in this recipe.

EACH SERVING PROVIDES
1145 kJ, 273 kcal, 28 g protein, 6 g fat
(2 g saturated fat), 26 g carbohydrate
(4 g sugars), <1 g fibre, 2061 mg sodium

# Quick & easy seafood soup

PREPARATION 10 minutes

COOKING 15 minutes

SERVES 4

## Cook's tips

● Use the best-looking marinara seafood mix you can find. Some fish shops sell a freshly made marinara mix, usually consisting of fresh chopped fish, calamari, prawns (shrimp) and mussels, flavoured with fresh herbs such as dill and parsley.

● Canned cherry tomatoes are used in this recipe, but if you can't find these, use canned chopped tomatoes instead.

EACH SERVING PROVIDES
995 kJ, 238 kcal, 33 g protein, 4 g fat
(1 g saturated fat), 9 g carbohydrate
(7 g sugars), 3 g fibre, 551 mg sodium

This is a cheat's version of bouillabaise, a classic French seafood soup that can take several hours to prepare.

**6 spring onions (scallions)**

**3 cloves garlic**

**¾ cup (180 ml) white wine**

**2 x 400 g (14 oz) cans cherry tomatoes in tomato juice**

**500 g (1 lb) seafood marinara mix (preferably one containing fresh herbs)**

1  Half-fill an electric kettle with water and bring to a boil.

2  Meanwhile, trim and slice the spring onions, and crush the garlic. Heat 1 tablespoon olive oil in a large saucepan over medium–high heat, then add the spring onions and garlic. Cook, stirring, for 2 minutes.

3  Increase the heat to high, add the wine and simmer for 2 minutes, or until reduced by half. Add 1 cup (250 ml) of the boiling water and the tomatoes in their juice, squashing some of the tomatoes with the back of a wooden spoon. Bring to a boil, then reduce the heat to medium and simmer for 4 minutes.

4  Add the marinara mix and simmer for 2 minutes, or until the seafood is just cooked. Season well with salt and freshly ground black pepper and serve.

## Variations

● Stir in some chopped fresh parsley or dill.
● For a spicy seafood soup, add chopped red chilli.

# Creamy cauliflower soup

PREPARATION 10 minutes

COOKING 15 minutes

SERVES 4–6

## Cook's tip

Using a hand-held stick blender to purée soup saves time and washing up. If you don't have one, you can purée soup in batches using a food processor. Allow the soup to cool a little first, to avoid hot splatters, and reheat gently before serving.

EACH SERVING PROVIDES
644 kJ, 154 kcal, 8 g protein, 8 g fat
(5 g saturated fat), 12 g carbohydrate
(11 g sugars), 6 g fibre, 1149 mg sodium

4 cups (1 litre) vegetable stock
1 cauliflower, about 1.5 kg (3 lb)
1 onion
½ cup (125 ml) pouring (light) cream
freshly ground nutmeg

1  Pour the stock into a saucepan; cover and bring to a boil.

2  Meanwhile, chop the cauliflower and onion. Heat 1½ tablespoons olive oil in a large saucepan over medium heat. Add the onion and cook, stirring, for 2–3 minutes, or until soft but not coloured.

3  Add the cauliflower and boiling stock. Cover and bring to a boil over high heat, then boil for 10–12 minutes, or until the cauliflower is tender.

4  Using a hand-held stick blender, purée the soup until smooth. Stir in the cream and briefly heat through. Season to taste with salt and freshly ground black pepper and ladle into serving bowls. Sprinkle with nutmeg and serve.

### Serving suggestion
This soup is delicious with fresh, crusty bread or a rustic loaf.

soups

# Pea & pesto soup

**750 g (1½ lb) frozen peas**
**4 spring onions (scallions)**
**1 tablespoon lime juice**
**2½ tablespoons pesto (see Basics)**

PREPARATION 10 minutes

COOKING 10 minutes

SERVES 4

1   Fill an electric kettle with water and bring to a boil. Pour 4 cups (1 litre) of the boiling water into a large saucepan and add the peas. Trim and discard the spring onion roots and tops, then add the spring onions to the pan. Cover and bring to a boil, then reduce the heat and simmer for 5 minutes.

2   Remove and discard the spring onions. Reserve about 1 cup (150 g) of the peas.

3   Add the lime juice and 1 tablespoon of the pesto to the remaining mixture. Using a hand-held stick blender, purée until smooth. Stir in the reserved peas, season well with salt and freshly ground black pepper and briefly reheat.

4   Ladle into serving bowls, top with the remaining pesto and serve.

## Shortcut ingredient
If you don't have time to make your own pesto, just use a good-quality ready-made pesto.

## Quick tip
When bringing a lot of liquid to a boil, cover the pan: the liquid will reach boiling point more quickly.

EACH SERVING PROVIDES
725 kJ, 173 kcal, 12 g protein, 9 g fat
(1 g saturated fat), 12 g carbohydrate
(4 g sugars), <1 g fibre, 35 mg sodium

**Serving suggestion**
Top with shaved parmesan or pecorino cheese or fresh basil leaves.

# Minestrone

PREPARATION 10 minutes

COOKING 15 minutes

SERVES 4

## Quick tip

First bringing the stock and tomatoes to a boil in a covered saucepan greatly shortens the cooking time in this recipe.

EACH SERVING PROVIDES
820 kJ, 196 kcal, 12 g protein, 1 g fat
(<1 g saturated fat), 34 g carbohydrate
(11 g sugars), 7 g fibre, 1627 mg sodium

2 x 410 g (15 oz) cans chopped tomatoes with basil,
 garlic and onion
4 cups (1 litre) chicken stock
⅔ cup (90 g) ditalini or macaroni, or any other short pasta
420 g (15 oz) can mixed beans
4 tablespoons chopped fresh parsley

1  Combine the tomatoes and stock in a large saucepan; cover and bring to a boil over high heat. Add the pasta and cook, uncovered, for 10 minutes, or until the pasta is al dente, stirring occasionally.

2  Meanwhile, drain and rinse the beans. Add to the soup and cook for 1 minute, or until heated through.

3  Stir in the parsley, season well with salt and freshly ground black pepper and serve.

### Serving suggestion
Serve sprinkled with parmesan, or with toasted ciabatta bread that has been sprinkled with parmesan and grilled (broiled) until golden.

## Variation

Add fried bacon or speck, or diced carrots, green beans, celery, potato or capsicum (bell pepper) to the soup.

# Pumpkin soup

**4 cups (1 litre) vegetable stock**
**1 onion**
**1.5 kg (3 lb) pumpkin (winter squash)**
**4 tablespoons chopped fresh coriander (cilantro)**
**4 tablespoons crème fraîche or sour cream**

1   Pour the stock into a saucepan; cover and bring to a boil. Meanwhile, chop the onion. Chop the pumpkin into 2 cm (¾ inch) cubes, removing the seeds and skin.

2   Heat 1½ tablespoons olive oil in a large saucepan over medium heat. Add the onion and cook, stirring, for 3 minutes, or until softened.

3   Add the pumpkin and the hot stock, then cover and bring to a boil over high heat. Boil for 10 minutes, or until the pumpkin is soft.

4   Using a hand-held stick blender, purée the mixture until smooth. Season to taste with salt and freshly ground black pepper and stir in most of the coriander. Ladle into serving bowls and top each with a spoonful of crème fraîche. Sprinkle with a little more black pepper, garnish with the remaining coriander and serve.

## Variations

● For a touch of spice, add about 3 teaspoons Moroccan spice mix (see Basics) or your favourite curry powder in step 2 when frying the onion.
● Replace the coriander with fresh chopped chives, or serve the soup sprinkled with grated nutmeg.

PREPARATION 10 minutes

COOKING 15 minutes

SERVES 6

## Cook's tip

Pumpkin soup freezes well, so if you have the time, make a double batch and freeze some in an airtight container for a quick meal during the week.

EACH SERVING PROVIDES
722 kJ, 172 kcal, 6 g protein, 7 g fat
(5 g saturated fat), 20 g carbohydrate
(14 g sugars), 3 g fibre, 923 mg sodium

# Creamy vichyssoise

PREPARATION 10 minutes

COOKING 15 minutes

SERVES 4

## Quick tip

Bringing the stock to a boil in a covered saucepan speeds the cooking time in this recipe.

## Variation

Add 2 crushed garlic cloves with the leeks and onion.

EACH SERVING PROVIDES
1059 kJ, 253 kcal, 7 g protein, 9 g fat (6 g saturated fat), 34 g carbohydrate (9 g sugars), 5 g fibre, 1392 mg sodium

**4 cups (1 litre) vegetable stock**

**2 leeks**

**1 onion**

**750 g (1½ lb) sebago or other all-purpose potatoes**

**½ cup (125 ml) pouring (light) cream**

1   Pour the stock into a saucepan; cover and bring to a boil. Meanwhile, trim the root and green leafy ends from the leeks, leaving only the white stems. Wash the stems well to remove any sand or grit, then cut in half lengthwise and thinly slice. Chop the onion. Peel the potatoes and cut into 3 cm (1¼ inch) cubes.

2   Heat 2 tablespoons olive oil in a large saucepan over medium–high heat. Add the leeks and onion and cook, stirring, for 3 minutes, or until the onion has softened.

3   Add the potatoes and boiling stock, then cover and bring to a boil. Reduce the heat to medium–low and simmer for 10 minutes, or until the potatoes are tender.

4   Using a hand-held stick blender, purée the mixture until smooth. Stir in the cream and briefly reheat. Season to taste with salt and freshly ground black pepper and serve.

# Creamy broccoli soup

PREPARATION 10 minutes

COOKING 15 minutes

SERVES 4–6

EACH SERVING PROVIDES
693 kJ, 165 kcal, 9 g protein, 8 g fat
(5 g saturated fat), 13 g carbohydrate
(6 g sugars), 8 g fibre, 1135 mg sodium

5 cups (1.25 litres) vegetable stock

800 g (1 lb 10 oz) broccoli

2 potatoes

1 onion

⅓ cup (80 ml) pouring (light) cream

1   Pour the stock into a saucepan; cover and bring to a boil.

2   Meanwhile, thinly slice the stem of the broccoli and cut the head into florets. Peel the potatoes and cut into small cubes. Chop the onion.

3   Heat 1 tablespoon olive oil in a large saucepan over medium heat. Add the onion and cook, stirring, for 2–3 minutes, or until softened. Add the broccoli, potatoes and hot stock. Bring back to a boil, then reduce the heat, cover and simmer for 10 minutes, or until the vegetables are tender.

4   Using a hand-held stick blender, purée the mixture until smooth. Stir in the cream and briefly reheat. Season to taste with salt and freshly ground black pepper, then ladle into serving bowls.

### Serving suggestion
Toasted cheese sandwiches would be lovely with this soup.

# Lentil & vegetable soup

PREPARATION 10 minutes

COOKING 15 minutes

SERVES 4

## Cook's tip

Use a frozen vegetable mix that contains small diced vegetables such as carrots, peas, swede (rutabaga), green beans and corn kernels — or instead of frozen vegetables use mixed diced fresh vegetables.

EACH SERVING PROVIDES
423 kJ, 103 kcal, 7 g protein, 6 g fat
(<1 g saturated fat), 15 g carbohydrate
(7 g sugars), 3 g fibre, 1568 mg sodium

This health-giving soup is very versatile, so feel free to substitute with any vegetables you have on hand. Instead of lentils you could also use chickpeas or your favourite canned beans.

**4 cups (1 litre) vegetable stock**

**1 potato**

**300 g (10 oz) mixed frozen vegetables**

**420 g (15 oz) can lentils**

**3 tablespoons chopped fresh parsley**

1  Pour the stock and 1 cup (250 ml) water into a large saucepan; cover and bring to a boil. Meanwhile, peel the potato and cut into small cubes.

2  Add the potato to the hot stock and boil for 4 minutes, then add the frozen vegetables and cook for a further 3–4 minutes, or until the vegetables are tender.

3  Meanwhile, drain and rinse the lentils. Add to the soup and cook for 1–2 minutes, or until heated through. Stir in the parsley, season to taste with freshly ground black pepper and serve.

**Serving suggestion**
Serve with slices of toasted sourdough or rustic bread.

# Fish laksa

500 g (1 lb) firm white fish fillets
150 g (5 oz) bean sprouts
200 g (7 oz) dried thin rice stick noodles
400 ml (14 fl oz) can light coconut milk
4 tablespoons laksa paste

PREPARATION 10 minutes
COOKING 15 minutes
SERVES 4

## Shopping tip

You can buy laksa paste from most supermarkets these days. Look for one containing spices such as galangal, lemongrass, chilli, garlic, turmeric and coriander and cumin seeds.

EACH SERVING PROVIDES
2059 kJ, 492 kcal, 30 g protein, 17 g fat (12 g saturated fat), 53 g carbohydrate (5 g sugars), 2 g fibre, 210 mg sodium

1  Fill an electric kettle with water and bring to a boil. Meanwhile, cut the fish into 2 cm (¾ inch) cubes and set aside. Trim any scraggly tails from the bean sprouts.

2  Pour the boiling water into a saucepan, refill the kettle and bring back to a boil. Add the noodles to the saucepan and bring to a boil over high heat. Reduce the heat a little and cook, stirring occasionally, for 5–8 minutes, or until the noodles are tender.

3  Meanwhile, pour 3 cups (750 ml) of the boiling water into another saucepan. Stir in the coconut milk and laksa paste. Bring back to a boil over high heat, then reduce the heat to medium–low. Cover and simmer for 5 minutes. Stir the fish into the laksa mixture and cook for 3–5 minutes, or until just firm and cooked. Remove from the heat.

4  Drain the noodles and divide among serving bowls. Ladle the fish and soup over the noodles, top with the bean sprouts and serve.

## Variations

- Add ⅓ cup (50 g) thawed frozen peas to the soup with the fish.
- Instead of the fish, use 500 g (1 lb) firm cubed tofu or sliced boneless, skinless chicken breast.
- Sprinkle with chopped red chilli and fresh herbs such as coriander (cilantro) and Vietnamese mint.

# Quick tom yum

## Quick tip

You can also use frozen peeled prawns in this soup. Add them to the hot soup while they are still frozen, and cook for about 6 minutes, or until they turn opaque and are cooked through.

EACH SERVING PROVIDES
592 kJ, 141 kcal, 21 g protein, 4 g fat
(1 g saturated fat), 4 g carbohydrate
(2 g sugars), 2 g fibre, 1052 mg sodium

100 g (3½ oz) snow peas (mangetout)
20 peeled raw prawns (uncooked shrimp)
2 tablespoons Thai tom yum soup paste
1 cup (90 g) bean sprouts
½ cup (15 g) fresh coriander (cilantro) leaves

1  Pour 6 cups (1.5 litres) water into a large saucepan; cover and bring to a boil. Meanwhile, thinly slice the snow peas.

2  Stir the tom yum paste into the boiling water until well combined. Add the prawns and cook for 2 minutes, then add the snow peas and cook for a further 2 minutes, or until the prawns are cooked.

3  Meanwhile, trim any scraggly tails from the bean sprouts. Add the bean sprouts to the soup, then ladle the soup into serving bowls. Garnish with the coriander and serve.

### Serving suggestion
Serve with lime wedges, for people to squeeze over their soup.

# Soba noodle soup

6 cups (1.5 litres) beef stock

180 g (6 oz) packet dried soba noodles

3–4 baby bok choy

1 long red chilli

1 tablespoon soy sauce

1  Pour the stock into a large saucepan; cover and bring to a boil. Add the noodles and cook for 4 minutes, or until tender.

2  Meanwhile, trim the bok choy, then separate the leaves and cut them in half. Thinly slice the chilli diagonally.

3  Add the bok choy to the stock and cook for 1–2 minutes, or until just wilted. Stir in the chilli and soy sauce and serve.

PREPARATION 10 minutes

COOKING 10 minutes

SERVES 4

## Cook's tip

Soba noodles are made with buckwheat flour and wheat flour. You'll find them in the Asian section of larger supermarkets.

EACH SERVING PROVIDES
925 kJ, 221 kcal, 15 g protein, 1 g fat (< 1 g saturated fat), 36 g carbohydrate (3 g sugars), 2 g fibre, 2650 mg sodium

# Spicy chorizo & bean soup

PREPARATION 10 minutes

COOKING 15 minutes

SERVES 4

## Cook's tip

If fresh basil isn't available, swirl some good-quality ready-made pesto through the soup.

EACH SERVING PROVIDES
677 kJ, 161 kcal, 10 g protein, 6 g fat
(2 g saturated fat), 16 g carbohydrate
(9 g sugars), 7 g fibre, 637 mg sodium

**2 chorizo sausages**

**1 red capsicum (bell pepper)**

**2 x 410 g (15 oz) cans chopped tomatoes**

**420 g (15 oz) can cannellini beans**

**3 tablespoons torn fresh basil**

1   Fill an electric kettle with water and bring to a boil. Meanwhile, cut the sausages in half lengthwise, then into 1 cm (½ inch) slices. Cut the capsicum into chunks.

2   Heat 2 teaspoons olive oil in a large saucepan over medium heat. Add the sausages and cook, stirring, for 3 minutes, or until golden brown. Add the capsicum and cook for a further 3 minutes, or until the capsicum has softened slightly.

3   Add the tomatoes and 3 cups (750 ml) of the boiling water. Cover and bring to a boil, then reduce the heat to medium and simmer for 5 minutes.

4   Meanwhile, drain and rinse the beans. Add to the soup and cook for 1–2 minutes, or until heated through. Stir in the basil and serve.

## Variations

- Use mixed canned beans instead of cannellini beans.
- Instead of fresh capsicum, use chargilled capsicum from a jar.
- Replace the chorizo with chopped bacon or speck.

# Pea soup with bacon

4 cups (1 litre) vegetable stock
1 onion
500 g (1 lb) potatoes
3 cups (465 g) frozen peas
4 rindless bacon slices (bacon strips)

1  Pour the stock into a saucepan; cover and bring to a boil. Meanwhile, chop the onion. Peel the potatoes and cut into small cubes.

2  Heat 2 tablespoons olive oil in a large saucepan over medium–high heat. Add the onion and cook, stirring, for 3 minutes, or until softened. Add the potatoes and hot stock. Cover and bring to a boil, then reduce the heat to medium–low and simmer for 5 minutes.

3  Stir in the peas and cook for a further 5 minutes, or until the potatoes are tender. Using a hand-held stick blender, purée the mixture until smooth.

4  While the soup is simmering, chop the bacon. Heat 1 tablespoon olive oil in a frying pan over medium–high heat and cook the bacon for 6–8 minutes, or until golden and crisp. Stir the bacon through the soup. Season with salt and freshly ground black pepper and serve.

**Serving suggestion**
This soup is excellent with crusty bread.

## Variations

- Add some crushed garlic when cooking the onion in step 2.
- Leave out the bacon and instead crumble some crisp fried prosciutto over the soup.

PREPARATION 10 minutes

COOKING 15 minutes

SERVES 4

## Cook's tip
Pea soup freezes well, so if you have the time, make a double batch and freeze some in an airtight container. It will keep for up to a month.

EACH SERVING PROVIDES
1039 kJ, 248 kcal, 20 g protein, 5 g fat (2 g saturated fat), 30 g carbohydrate (8 g sugars), 2 g fibre, 2011 mg sodium

starters, light meals
& snacks

# Pizza pizzazz!

Few can resist a slice of hot fresh pizza. Pizzas can be so quick to prepare and cook and are a great way to feed the multitudes.

## Choose your pizza base

If you have time, try making your own pizza dough using the recipe given here. Why not make a double batch of dough, then divide the extra dough into two portions and freeze in airtight snap-lock bags for your next pizza meal? The dough can be frozen for up to 1 month.

If you don't have time to wait for dough to prove, whip up a basic scone dough, roll it out thinly and use that as your pizza base (crust).

Alternatively, stock up on any of the commercial pizza bases (crusts) available at the supermarket and keep them in the freezer. At a pinch, you can also use flat pita bread, or pide (Turkish flat bread) split in half horizontally, as a pizza base (crust).

## Homemade pizza dough

PREPARATION 10 minutes + 10 minutes resting + 45 minutes proving   COOKING 10 minutes   MAKES two pizzas

**2 teaspoons dry (powdered) yeast**
**1 teaspoon caster (superfine) sugar**
**1 teaspoon salt**
**2 cups (300 g) plain (all-purpose) flour**
**2 tablespoons olive oil**

Combine the yeast, sugar and salt in a small bowl with ¾ cup (180 ml) lukewarm water. Leave to stand for 10 minutes, or until frothy.

Place the flour in a large bowl and make a well in the centre. Pour in the yeast mixture, then mix together until combined. Gather the dough into a ball and knead on a lightly floured surface for 5 minutes.

Place the dough in a lightly oiled bowl, cover with a clean tea towel (dish towel) and leave in a warm place for 45 minutes, or until doubled in size. Punch down the dough, then divide in half. Roll each portion out to a 22 cm (8½ inch) round and place on two lightly oiled pizza trays.

Add your favourite topping and bake at 200°C (400°F/Gas 6) for 10 minutes, or until the base is crisp and golden and the topping is bubbling.

# Choose your topping

The topping quantities given below are sufficient for two 22 cm (8½ inch) pizzas.

## Basic margherita

½ cup (125 g) tomato pizza sauce
150 g (5 oz) sliced bocconcini (fresh baby
  mozzarella balls)
4 tablespoons fresh basil leaves

Spread the bases with the pizza sauce. Top with the cheese and bake as directed. Serve scattered with basil leaves.

## Seafood

½ cup (125 g) tomato pizza sauce
200 g (7 oz) seafood marinara mix (see note)
⅔ cup (90 g) grated mozzarella
2 tablespoons chopped fresh parsley

Spread the bases with the pizza sauce. Drain the marinara mix and arrange over the bases. Sprinkle with the cheese and bake as directed. Serve sprinkled with the parsley.

**NOTE** You can use any raw prepared seafood, such as small prawns (shrimp), scallops, mussels and fish fillet pieces.

### Cook's tip

Tomato pasta sauce usually has a better flavour than products labelled 'pizza sauce'. Use a ready-made sauce, or our Super-easy Tomato Sauce on page 212.

## Ham & pineapple

225 g (8 oz) can pineapple pieces
200 g (7 oz) sliced ham
½ cup (125 g) tomato pizza sauce
1 cup (100 g) grated cheddar

Drain the pineapple and chop the ham. Spread the bases with the pizza sauce. Arrange the ham and pineapple over the bases. Sprinkle with the cheese and bake as directed.

## Spicy salami

125 g (4 oz) sliced spicy salami
1 small red capsicum (bell pepper)
½ cup (125 g) tomato pizza sauce
1 cup (125 g) grated mozzarella

Roughly chop the salami and slice the capsicum. Spread the bases with the pizza sauce. Arrange the salami and capsicum over the bases. Sprinkle with the cheese and bake as directed.

## Antipasto

125 g (4 oz) marinated quartered artichoke hearts
100 g (3½ oz) marinated semi-dried (sun-blushed)
  tomatoes
⅓ cup (80 g) pesto (see Basics)
150 g (5 oz) sliced bocconcini (fresh baby
  mozzarella balls)

Drain any excess marinade from the artichokes and tomatoes. Spread the bases with the pesto. Arrange the artichokes, tomatoes and cheese over the bases, then bake as directed.

## Gourmet vegetarian

½ cup (125 g) tomato pizza sauce
100 g (3½ oz) roasted red capsicum (bell pepper),
  cut into strips
1 cup (45 g) baby English spinach leaves
125 g (4 oz) fetta

Spread the bases with the pizza sauce. Chop the capsicum and arrange over the bases, then top with the spinach leaves. Crumble the fetta all over and bake as directed. Serve drizzled with a little extra virgin olive oil.

# Spicy prawns with raita

PREPARATION 10 minutes

COOKING 5 minutes

SERVES 4

## Cook's tip

Garam masala is a traditional Indian blend of ground dried spices. It is available from supermarkets and specialty food shops.

## Quick tip

The raita can be made up to 1 day in advance. Cover and refrigerate until required.

EACH SERVING PROVIDES
611 kJ, 146 kcal, 25 g protein, 3 g fat
(1 g saturated fat), 3 g carbohydrate
(2 g sugars), <1 g fibre, 192 mg sodium

½ cup (125 g) natural (plain) yogurt

3 tablespoons fresh mint leaves

24 large peeled raw prawns (uncooked shrimp), tails on

½ teaspoon garam masala

½ teaspoon chilli powder

1   To make the raita, combine the yogurt and mint in a small food processor and blend until the mint is finely chopped. Transfer to a bowl, season to taste with a little salt and garnish with extra mint.

2   Meanwhile, preheat a chargrill pan, heavy-based frying pan or barbecue to high heat. Put the prawns in a bowl, sprinkle with the garam masala and chilli powder, then drizzle with 1 tablespoon olive oil and toss to coat.

3   Cook the prawns for 2 minutes on each side, or until they have become opaque and lightly golden. Serve immediately, with the raita on the side for dipping.

### Serving suggestion

This is a good starter for a casual barbecue. If you want to dress the dish up a bit, you could plate the prawns on a bed of baby rocket (arugula) or salad leaves and drizzle with the raita. Garnish the prawns or raita with extra mint leaves if desired.

### Variation

Substitute scallops for the prawns, or use a combination of both. If using both, thread them alternately onto skewers for ease of handling, and for a lovely presentation.

# Fetta, pesto & tomato tarts

200 g (7 oz) cherry tomatoes
1 sheet frozen puff pastry, thawed
⅓ cup (90 g) pesto (see Basics)
⅓ cup (50 g) crumbled fetta
½ cup (20 g) baby rocket (arugula) leaves

PREPARATION 10 minutes

COOKING 15 minutes

SERVES 4

EACH SERVING PROVIDES
1394 kJ, 333 kcal, 7 g protein, 27 g fat
(9 g saturated fat), 16 g carbohydrate
(2 g sugars), 2 g fibre, 385 mg sodium

1  Preheat the oven to 200°C (400°F/Gas 6). Line two baking trays with baking (parchment) paper. Cut the cherry tomatoes in half.

2  Cut the pastry into quarters. Cut a 1 cm (½ inch) strip from each side of each square. Press the strips back onto each pastry square, to make a rim around the edge, trimming to fit. Place them all on one baking tray, then prick the centres all over with a fork.

3  On the other tray, arrange the tomatoes, cut side up. Bake the pastry and tomatoes (with the pastry on the top shelf) for 15 minutes.

4  Remove from the oven and cool slightly. If the pastry centres have puffed up, press them down with the back of a spoon. Spread the pesto into each tart, top with the tomatoes, fetta and rocket and serve.

# Fig & prosciutto salad

**PREPARATION** 10 minutes

**COOKING** none

**SERVES** 4

## Shopping tip
Balsamic glaze is a thick and sweet balsamic vinegar reduction. You'll find it in supermarkets, in the salad dressing aisle.

EACH SERVING PROVIDES
637 kJ, 152 kcal, 11 g protein, 9 g fat (5 g saturated fat), 6 g carbohydrate (6 g sugars), 2 g fibre, 494 mg sodium

**6 fresh figs**
**8 slices of prosciutto**
**1⅓ cups (60 g) baby rocket (arugula) leaves**
**60 g (2 oz) blue cheese**
**balsamic glaze, for drizzling**

1  Cut the figs into quarters. Tear each prosciutto slice into 4–6 pieces.

2  Arrange the rocket, figs and prosciutto on serving plates.

3  Crumble the blue cheese over the top, then drizzle with a little extra virgin olive oil and the balsamic glaze. Sprinkle with freshly ground black pepper and serve.

### Serving suggestion
This salad makes a lovely starter, or you could increase the quantities slightly and serve with crusty bread for lunch.

# Tomato & hummus bruschetta

3 ripe tomatoes

½ small red onion

8 thick slices of sourdough or crusty bread

⅔ cup (140 g) hummus (see Basics)

4 tablespoons baby basil leaves or torn fresh basil

1  Dice the tomatoes and finely dice the onion. Combine in a small bowl and season to taste with salt and freshly ground black pepper.

2  Toast the bread on both sides, then spread the toasts with hummus.

3  Place on serving plates and spoon the tomato mixture on top. Scatter with the basil, drizzle with extra virgin olive oil if desired and serve.

**PREPARATION** 10 minutes

**COOKING** 5 minutes

**SERVES** 4

## Cook's tip

If your loaf of bread is large, use only four slices.

EACH SERVING PROVIDES
1108 kJ, 265 kcal, 11 g protein, 8 g fat
(1 g saturated fat), 37 g carbohydrate
(5 g sugars), 8 g fibre, 492 mg sodium

starters, light meals & snacks

# Mini pancakes

These pancakes are perfect for an impromptu snack or to serve with drinks. For a dainty presentation, make them half the size.

1 cup (150 g) self-raising flour
⅔ cup (150 ml) milk
1 egg
200 g (7 oz) smoked salmon
200 g (7 oz) spreadable cream cheese

1 Put the flour in a bowl and make a well in the centre. Whisk the milk and egg together until combined, then pour into the flour. Stir gently with the whisk until smooth — do not overbeat, or the pancakes will be tough.

2 Heat a large heavy-based frying pan over medium heat, then lightly oil it. Using 1 level tablespoon of batter for each pancake, drop spoonfuls of batter into the pan. Depending on the size of your pan, you should be able to cook four pancakes at a time; they should each spread to about 6–7 cm (2½–2¾ inches).

3 Cook for 1 minute, or until bubbles appear on the surface. Turn and cook for a further 30 seconds to 1 minute, or until golden brown underneath. Remove to a plate and cook the remaining batter.

4 Chop or slice the smoked salmon. Spread the pancakes with cream cheese and top with the salmon. Serve warm or at room temperature.

## Variations
- Mix chopped fresh herbs through the batter, and top with sliced ham or roast beef and half a cherry tomato.
- For a sweet treat, top with a dollop of thick (heavy/double) cream and half a strawberry, serve with butter and honey or jam, or serve hot with maple syrup and ice cream.

PREPARATION 10 minutes

COOKING 15 minutes

MAKES 24

## Quick tip
If you happen to have any pancakes left over, sandwich two pancakes together with your favourite topping and pack for lunchtime snacks.

EACH PANCAKE PROVIDES
282 kJ, 67 kcal, 4 g protein, 4 g fat (2 g saturated fat), 5 g carbohydrate (<1 g sugars), <1 g fibre, 226 mg sodium

starters, light meals & snacks

# Mushroom omelettes

**PREPARATION** 10 minutes

**COOKING** 10 minutes

**SERVES** 2

## Shortcut ingredient

Buy pre-sliced button mushrooms to save some chopping time.

## Cook's tip

Kecap manis is a thick, sweet Indonesian-style soy sauce. Use oyster sauce if you prefer.

EACH SERVING PROVIDES
714 kJ, 170 kcal, 15 g protein, 10 g fat
(3 g saturated fat), 5 g carbohydrate
(4 g sugars), 2 g fibre, 365 mg sodium

**3 spring onions (scallions)**

**100 g (3½ oz) mixed mushrooms**

**4 eggs**

**2 teaspoons kecap manis**

**1 tablespoon chopped fresh coriander (cilantro)**

1  Finely slice the spring onions and mushrooms. Heat 2 teaspoons vegetable oil in a non-stick frying pan measuring 18 cm (7 inches) across the base. Cook the spring onions and mushrooms over medium heat for 5 minutes, or until just softened. Remove to a plate.

2  Wipe the frying pan clean, then heat another 1 teaspoon oil over medium heat. In a bowl, whisk the eggs with a fork, then pour half the egg mixture into the pan, swirling to coat the base. Draw the egg from the side of the pan to the centre as the omelette cooks, letting the uncooked egg run out to the side. Cook for 1 minute, or until set underneath but still runny on top.

3  Sprinkle half the mushroom mixture across the centre of the omelette. Fold one-third of the omelette towards the centre, then over again to enclose the filling. Slide onto a plate, drizzle with half the kecap manis and sprinkle with half the coriander. Keep warm.

4  Repeat to make another omelette. Serve hot.

## Variations

Make the basic omelettes, but instead try the following fillings:
- sautéed baby spinach leaves, crumbled fetta and fresh chopped dill
- sliced ham, chopped tomato and grated cheddar
- cooked baby prawns (shrimp) and/or crabmeat
- smoked salmon, creamy goat's cheese and fresh chopped parsley.

# Savoury egg scramble

**PREPARATION** 10 minutes

**COOKING** 10 minutes

**SERVES** 4

## Variation

Serve the scrambled eggs on toasted bread, or wrapped in warmed tortillas.

EACH SERVING PROVIDES
1172 kJ, 280 kcal, 21 g protein, 10 g fat
(3 g saturated fat), 25 g carbohydrate
(3 g sugars), 3 g fibre, 688 mg sodium

**2 rindless bacon slices (bacon strips)**

**1 small red capsicum (bell pepper)**

**4 spring onions (scallions)**

**6 eggs**

**4 split English muffins**

1 Chop the bacon and capsicum, and slice the spring onions.

2 Heat 2 teaspoons olive oil in a large, deep, non-stick frying pan over medium heat. Add the bacon, capsicum and spring onions and cook for 5 minutes, or until the capsicum is soft and lightly browned.

3 In a bowl, lightly whisk the eggs with a fork. Pour the egg mixture into the pan and cook for about 3 minutes, folding the mixture in from the edge to the centre to create large curds. Don't overcook, as the eggs will keep cooking in their own heat.

4 Meanwhile, lightly toast the muffins. Serve the eggs immediately, with or on top of the toasted muffins.

# Poached eggs on Turkish toast

**3 ripe tomatoes**

**3 spring onions (scallions)**

**½ teaspoon ground sumac or paprika, plus extra for sprinkling**

**4 eggs**

**½ Turkish bread loaf**

**PREPARATION** 10 minutes

**COOKING** 5 minutes

**SERVES** 4

### Cook's tip

Sumac is a berry used in Middle Eastern cuisine. It has a slightly tangy citrus flavour and is sold in ground form in many large supermarkets and specialty food stores.

EACH SERVING PROVIDES
836 kJ, 200 kcal, 11 g protein, 6 g fat (2 g saturated fat), 24 g carbohydrate (3 g sugars), 3 g fibre, 316 mg sodium

1   Bring a large shallow saucepan or deep frying pan of water to a boil over high heat. Meanwhile, dice the tomatoes and finely slice the spring onions. Combine in a small bowl with the sumac and season to taste with salt and freshly ground black pepper.

2   Reduce the heat to low, so the water is at a gentle simmer. Working one at a time, crack the eggs into a teacup and slide them into the water. Poach for 3–4 minutes, or until the whites have set.

3   Meanwhile, split the bread horizontally, then cut it crosswise to make four square pieces. Toast each piece on both sides.

4   Remove the eggs from the pan with a slotted spoon and drain the water off. Place one egg on each Turkish toast and spoon the tomato mixture on top. Sprinkle with extra sumac and serve immediately.

starters, light meals & snacks

# Maple French toast

PREPARATION 10 minutes

COOKING 15 minutes

SERVES 4

## Cook's tip

Thick pre-sliced bread will do, but this dish is even nicer made with thick slices cut from a rustic-style loaf. Make sure the bread is at least a day old, as this will help it absorb the egg mixture more readily.

EACH SERVING PROVIDES
1857 kJ, 444 kcal, 18 g protein, 20 g fat (9 g saturated fat), 48 g carbohydrate (13 g sugars), 2 g fibre, 603 mg sodium

**6 eggs**

**1 cup (250 ml) milk**

**2 tablespoons maple syrup, plus extra to serve**

**8 thick slices of day-old bread**

**2 tablespoons butter**

1   In a bowl, whisk the eggs, milk and maple syrup together with a fork. Pour the batter into a shallow dish large enough to hold the bread in a single layer — you may need to use two separate dishes. Lay the bread slices in the dish and leave to soak for 5 minutes, turning once.

2   Melt half the butter in a large non-stick frying pan over medium–low heat. Cook half the bread slices for 2–3 minutes on each side, or until the bread is lightly browned and the egg has set. Remove from the pan and keep warm.

3   Cook the remaining bread slices in the remaining butter. Serve immediately, drizzled with extra maple syrup.

## Serving suggestion
Top with seasonal sliced fresh fruit, such as strawberries, bananas, peaches or nectarines.

# Quesadillas

Even kids love quesadillas! Experiment with other fillings, but don't be tempted to overfill the quesadillas — they need to be quite thin so they don't fall apart.

**250 g (8 oz) cheddar**

**3 spring onions (scallions)**

**4 tablespoons chopped fresh coriander (cilantro)**

**8 flour tortillas, about 20 cm (8 inches) in diameter**

**⅔ cup (170 g) Mexican-style tomato salsa**

1 Grate the cheese into a bowl. Finely slice the spring onions and mix through the cheese with the coriander. Lay four tortillas on a clean surface and evenly sprinkle with the cheese mixture. Place another tortilla on top of each one.

2 Heat a frying pan over medium heat, then lightly oil. Carefully place a quesadilla into the pan and cook for about 1½ minutes, or until the tortilla is lightly golden underneath and the cheese has started to melt.

3 Turn the tortilla over and cook the other side for about 1½ minutes, then transfer to a chopping board. Cook the remaining quesadillas in the same way.

4 Cut the quesadillas into wedges and serve drizzled with a little salsa.

## Variations

Try these alternative fillings:
- a small amount of shredded cooked chicken, chopped salami or ham
- mashed canned refried beans or red kidney beans, mixed with a ready-made taco sauce
- thinly sliced Chinese barbecued pork, drizzled with hoisin or barbecue sauce.

**PREPARATION** 10 minutes

**COOKING** 15 minutes

**SERVES** 4

## Quick tip

To speed things up, have two frying pans on the go at once.

EACH SERVING PROVIDES
1728 kJ, 413 kcal, 20 g protein, 23 g fat
(14 g saturated fat), 31 g carbohydrate
(5 g sugars), 5 g fibre, 725 mg sodium

# Sweet potato chips

peanut or vegetable oil, for deep-frying
400 g (14 oz) orange sweet potatoes
2 teaspoons sea salt
½ teaspoon dried rosemary

1   Half-fill a large saucepan with oil and heat over high heat.

2   Meanwhile, using a mortar and pestle, spice grinder, or the end of a rolling pin in a small bowl, crush the salt and rosemary together until combined. Peel the sweet potato, then use a vegetable peeler to shave the flesh into long strips.

3   Cook the sweet potato strips in four batches, for about 1½ minutes each batch, until lightly browned.

4   Drain on paper towels; the chips will become crisp on cooling. Sprinkle with the rosemary salt and serve.

## Variation
Sprinkle the sweet potato chips with salt and your favourite hot spice mix, or even ground cinnamon mixed with brown sugar.

PREPARATION 10 minutes

COOKING 10 minutes

SERVES 4–6

## Quick tip
If you have one, you could use a mandoline to slice the sweet potato. A mandoline is a simple gadget used by chefs to quickly slice vegetables into uniformly thin discs or julienne strips. Some mandolines also have a crinkle-cut attachment.

EACH SERVING PROVIDES
765 kJ, 183 kcal, 2 g protein, 15 g fat (2 g saturated fat), 11 g carbohydrate (4 g sugars), 1 g fibre, 977 mg sodium

# Cheese & chive scones

PREPARATION 10 minutes

COOKING 15 minutes

MAKES 15

## Cook's tip

When mixing and rolling the scone dough, it is important to handle it as lightly as possible, otherwise the scones will be dry and tough.

## Shortcut ingredient

To save some time and washing up, you can buy cheddar that has already been grated.

EACH SCONE PROVIDES
644 kJ, 154 kcal, 5 g protein, 7 g fat (4 g saturated fat), 18 g carbohydrate (<1 g sugars), 1 g fibre, 261 mg sodium

2½ cups (375 g) self-raising flour

3 tablespoons butter, plus extra for spreading

1¼ cups (125 g) pre-grated cheddar

2 tablespoons chopped fresh chives

¾ cup (180 ml) milk, plus extra for brushing

1   Preheat the oven to 200°C (400°F/Gas 6). Line a baking tray with baking (parchment) paper.

2   Meanwhile, sift the flour into a large bowl. Chop the butter. Using your fingertips, rub the butter into the flour until evenly combined. Stir in the cheese and chives, then make a well in the centre. Mix in the milk using a flat-bladed knife until evenly moistened (you may need to add another tablespoon of milk — no more), then gather the dough together with your hands.

3   Turn the dough out onto a lightly floured surface and gently press out to a 2 cm (¾ inch) thickness, using the heel of your hand. Use a 5 cm (2 inch) round cutter to cut rounds from the dough, as close together as possible to get the most scones from the first rolling. Gently press the dough scraps together, lightly re-roll them, then cut out more scones.

4   Place the scones on the baking tray, just touching each other. Brush the tops lightly with a little extra milk. Bake for 15 minutes, or until risen and golden brown. Serve warm, spread with extra butter.

## Serving suggestion

These scones are great just as they are, or spread with butter. Also try them as an accompaniment to soups or stews.

# Little raspberry muffins

**PREPARATION** 10 minutes

**COOKING** 15 minutes

**MAKES** 24

## Variations

● Use frozen blueberries instead of raspberries.
● Add 1 teaspoon vanilla extract or finely grated orange zest to the batter.

EACH MUFFIN PROVIDES
173 kJ, 41 kcal, 1 g protein, 1 g fat
(<1 g saturated fat), 7 g carbohydrate
(2 g sugars), <1 g fibre, 49 mg sodium

1 cup (150 g) self-raising flour

⅓ cup (40 g) icing (confectioners') sugar, plus extra for dusting

⅔ cup (160 g) light sour cream

1 egg

1 cup (125 g) frozen raspberries, unthawed, roughly chopped

1  Preheat the oven to 180°C (350°F/Gas 4). Lightly grease a 24-hole mini muffin tin, or line the holes with paper cases.

2  Sift the flour and sugar into a bowl, then make a well in the centre.

3  In another bowl, whisk the sour cream, egg and ¼ cup (60 ml) water with a fork. Add to the dry ingredients and fold together until almost combined, then fold in the raspberries.

4  Divide the mixture evenly among the muffin holes. Bake for 15 minutes, or until the muffins have risen and are springy to a gentle touch. Dust lightly with icing sugar and serve warm, or cool on a wire rack. These muffins can also be frozen for up to 2 weeks.

# Currant cookies

125 g (4 oz) butter, at room temperature, chopped

1 cup (185 g) soft brown sugar

1 egg

1½ cups (225 g) plain (all-purpose) flour

½ cup (100 g) currants

**PREPARATION** 10 minutes

**COOKING** 15 minutes

**MAKES** about 30

## Quick tip

Just measure out the first tablespoon of dough — after that you can pinch off pieces of dough roughly the same size.

EACH COOKIE PROVIDES
349 kJ, 83 kcal, 1 g protein, 4 g fat
(2 g saturated fat), 12 g carbohydrate
(6 g sugars), <1 g fibre, 33 mg sodium

1   Preheat the oven to 180°C (350°F/Gas 4). Line two baking trays with baking (parchment) paper.

2   Using electric beaters, beat the butter and sugar until light and creamy. Beat in the egg, then use a flat-bladed knife to mix in the flour and currants until evenly combined.

3   Take level tablespoons of the dough and place on the baking trays. Flatten slightly with a spoon, or using your fingers, then bake for 12 minutes, or until golden brown underneath, swapping the trays around halfway through baking so they brown evenly.

4   Cool on the baking trays for 3 minutes, then transfer to a wire rack to cool completely. Store for up to 3 days in an airtight container.

salads

# Sensational salads

Brilliantly simple to toss together, the humble salad offers endless scope for creativity. Side salads are a cinchy way to add seasonal colour and texture to a meal, while other salads are substantial enough to enjoy as a healthy meal on their own.

## Super salad combos

Create the perfect balance of flavours and textures by combining seasonal fresh produce and perhaps a pantry staple or two, tossed through with a dressing of your choice. You can easily turn a side salad into a main by adding a protein or grain component. Here are a few ideas to start you thinking.

● **Vegetables** – choose the freshest seasonal produce, in an array of colours, textures and flavours.

● **Protein** – add some cooked poultry, meats and seafood, such as tuna, salmon and prawns (shrimp).

● **Grains & legumes** – add some cooked pasta, rice, noodles, couscous, chickpeas, lentils, tofu, corn and canned beans, such as cannellini or mixed beans.

● **For extra flavour & texture** – toss in some choice items such as capers, olives or gherkins (pickles); canned artichokes; crisp croutons; toasted nuts, sunflower seeds, sesame seeds or pepitas (pumpkin seeds); crisp fried bacon, prosciutto or pancetta; crumbled fetta, blue cheese or grated parmesan.

### Secrets of a great salad

● Salads are usually best made just before serving, although most dressings can be made a day ahead.

● Before adding them to a salad, briefly blanch any hard vegetables (such as broccoli) first, then briefly plunge them in cold water to retain their colour and to quickly stop them cooking.

● For added flavour and sweetness, toss in some fruit, such as cranberries, tangerine sections, sliced strawberries, apple slices or red grapes.

● Instead of a dressing, simply drizzle a salad with a flavoured oil, such as hazelnut, walnut or avocado.

● A salad that contains a variety of fruits and vegetables may not need any dressing at all — just a fresh squeeze of lemon, lime or orange juice.

## A splash of dash

Salad dressings are so versatile, but generally they contain an oil, an acidic element and any number of flavourings. Experiment with your own substitutions and additions — you can't really go wrong.

● **Oil** – try extra virgin and olive oil, or a flavoured oil such as walnut, hazelnut, avocado and sesame.

● **Acid** – choose from a vinegar such as balsamic, cider, white or red wine vinegar, rice wine or sushi vinegar; citrus juice, such as lemon, lime or orange juice; verjuice (juice of unripe grapes).

● **Flavours** – add a pinch of salt or a splash of soy or fish sauce; sweeten the dressing with a little sugar, honey or palm sugar (jaggery); add spices such as garlic, ginger, chillies, mustard or wasabi; and fresh or dried herbs such as thyme, lemon thyme, sage, tarragon, lemon myrtle, lemongrass and finely shredded makrut (kaffir lime) leaves.

# 7 super salad dressings

**Classic vinaigrette** Combine 2 tablespoons lemon juice or balsamic vinegar and 3 tablespoons olive oil and season with salt and pepper.

**VARIATION** Add ½ teaspoon caster (superfine) sugar and some fresh or dried herbs.

**French dressing** Combine 1 tablespoon red wine vinegar, 3 tablespoons extra virgin olive oil, 1 teaspoon caster (superfine) sugar, 1 teaspoon dijon mustard and 1 teaspoon salt.

**Asian dressing** Combine 2 tablespoons lemon juice, 2 tablespoons soy sauce, 2 teaspoons sesame oil and 2 teaspoons grated fresh ginger.

**OPTIONAL** Add 1 teaspoon fish sauce.

**Mustard dressing** Combine 2 tablespoons olive oil, 2 tablespoons white wine vinegar and 1 tablespoon wholegrain mustard and season with salt and pepper.

**Oil-free dressing** Combine 2 tablespoons rice vinegar, 1 tablespoon caster (superfine) sugar and ½ teaspoon salt.

**Thousand island dressing** Combine ½ cup (125 g) mayonnaise, 2 tablespoons tomato paste (concentrated purée), 2 tablespoons tomato sauce (ketchup), 2 teaspoons worcestershire sauce and ¼ teaspoon Tabasco sauce.

**Hummus dressing** Dilute some hummus (see Basics, page 312) with orange juice, lemon juice or water to the preferred consistency.

# Marvellous ways with mayo

There are endless ways to jazz up mayonnaise, whether you're whipping your mayo up from scratch (see Basics, page 308), or using some from a jar. Add the following ingredients to 1 cup (250 g) mayo.

- **Herb** ½ cup chopped mixed fresh herbs, such as chives, parsley, basil, thyme
- **Mustard** 1 tablespoon dijon mustard
- **Lime or lemon** 2 teaspoons grated zest and 1 tablespoon juice
- **Curry** 1 tablespoon curry powder
- **Horseradish** 2 tablespoons ready-made horseradish and 2 tablespoons finely snipped fresh chives

**COOK'S TIP** If you prefer, you can use 125 g (4 oz) mayo mixed with 125 g (4 oz) natural (plain) yogurt, sour cream or crème fraîche.

Left to right: hummus dressing, thousand island dressing, oil-free dressing, mustard dressing, Asian dressing, French dressing, classic vinaigrette.

# Apple fennel salad with toasted hazelnuts

**2 tablespoons lemon juice**
**2 small fennel bulbs, about 225 g (8 oz) each, with fronds**
**1 large red apple**
**2 cups (60 g) watercress sprigs**
**⅓ cup (45 g) toasted hazelnuts**

1   Whisk the lemon juice with 3 tablespoons extra virgin olive oil and some salt and freshly ground black pepper.

2   Trim the root end from the fennel bulbs, reserving the fronds as a garnish. Cut the fennel bulbs into quarters, then thinly slice and place in a large salad bowl.

3   Cut the apple into quarters and remove the seeds. Thinly slice the apple quarters, leaving the skin on for added colour. Add to the fennel with the watercress and hazelnuts.

4   Drizzle with the lemon dressing and toss well. Garnish with the reserved fennel fronds and serve.

## Variations

- For a more substantial salad, add some cooked prawns (shrimp), or some barbecued or smoked chicken.
- Add ⅓ cup (35 g) shredded or shaved parmesan.
- Substitute other nuts.
- Use green apples, or use half a green one and half a red one, leaving the skin on for extra colour.

PREPARATION 10 minutes

COOKING none

SERVES 4

## Cook's tip

Toasted hazelnuts are available from selected supermarkets, but it is easy to toast your own. Place the nuts in a frying pan without any oil and fry over medium heat until golden, stirring occasionally. Wrap in a clean cloth and rub to remove the skins. Keep the hazelnuts in the cloth and gently hit with a meat mallet to coarsely crush them.

EACH SERVING PROVIDES
520 kJ, 124 kcal, 4 g protein, 7 g fat (<1 g saturated fat), 11 g carbohydrate (11 g sugars), 6 g fibre, 51 mg sodium

# Warm potato salad

PREPARATION 10 minutes

COOKING 15 minutes

SERVES 4

## Shopping tip

When buying potatoes, check to see how they are labelled. 'Boiling', 'waxy' or 'salad' potatoes are good for salads as they hold their shape well when boiled. 'Starchy', 'floury', 'baking' or 'mashing' potatoes are best for roasting or mashing due to their higher starch content. Potatoes labelled 'all-purpose' are good all-rounders.

EACH SERVING PROVIDES
790 kJ, 189 kcal, 12 g protein, 4 g fat (1 g saturated fat), 25 g carbohydrate (9 g sugars), 2 g fibre, 642 mg sodium

500 g (1 lb) boiling (waxy) potatoes, such as desiree

4 rindless bacon slices (bacon strips)

2 spring onions (scallions)

¼ cup (60 ml) white wine vinegar

2 tablespoons sugar

1   Fill an electric kettle with water and bring to a boil. Wash the potatoes and dice them, leaving the skin on if preferred. Place in a saucepan and cover with boiling water. Gently boil for 8–10 minutes, or until just tender when pierced with a knife.

2   Meanwhile, dice the bacon. Chop the spring onions and set aside. Heat a non-stick frying pan over medium–high heat and fry the bacon in a little olive oil for 5 minutes, or until crisp. Remove from the pan and set aside.

3   Add the vinegar, sugar, ½ teaspoon salt and some freshly ground black pepper to the pan and bring to a boil. Pour the mixture into a heatproof cup and whisk in 2 tablespoons olive oil.

4   Drain the potatoes and place in a large salad bowl. Add the spring onions, dressing and bacon and gently toss to combine. Serve warm.

## Variations

●   For a creamy salad, cool the cooked potato, then toss with about ⅓ cup (85 g) good-quality mayonnaise, or mayonnaise mixed with natural (plain) yogurt.
●   Add 1–2 boiled eggs, peeled and cut into quarters, or cooked diced chicken or prawns (shrimp).
●   Substitute spicy chorizo sausage for the bacon.
●   Toss through some chopped fresh flat-leaf parsley, thinly sliced celery, cooked green peas, or a diced green pear with the skin on.

# Easy niçoise salad

PREPARATION 10 minutes

COOKING 10 minutes

SERVES 4

## Variations

● Add a few cooked small new potatoes, cut in half.
● Add blanched green beans and halved baby truss tomatoes.

EACH SERVING PROVIDES
2067 kJ, 494 kcal, 49 g protein, 32 g fat (6 g saturated fat), 3 g carbohydrate (<1 g sugars), <1 g fibre, 1076 mg sodium

**4 eggs**

**2 x 425 g (15 oz) cans chunky tuna in olive oil**

**2 baby cos (romaine) lettuces**

**½ cup (95 g) kalamata olives**

**2 tablespoons red wine vinegar**

1  Place the eggs in a small saucepan of cold water and bring to a boil over high heat. Reduce the heat to medium and gently boil, uncovered, for 7 minutes, stirring occasionally. Drain and cool under cold running water. Allow the eggs to cool, then peel and cut into quarters.

2  Drain the tuna, reserving the oil. Separate the lettuce leaves. Layer the lettuce, tuna, olives and egg quarters in a large salad bowl.

3  Whisk the vinegar with 2 tablespoons of reserved tuna oil (add some extra virgin olive oil if needed), plus some salt and freshly ground black pepper. Pour over the salad, toss together and serve.

salads

# Bocconcini tomato salad

300 g (10 oz) bocconcini (fresh baby mozzarella balls)

400 g (14 oz) truss tomatoes

16 fresh basil leaves

¼ cup (40 g) toasted pine nuts

1½ tablespoons balsamic vinegar

1  Cut the bocconcini and tomatoes into slices. Arrange the bocconcini and tomato slices on a serving plate.

2  Roughly tear the basil leaves. Scatter the basil and pine nuts over the salad.

3  Whisk the vinegar with 2 tablespoons extra virgin olive oil and some salt and freshly ground black pepper. Drizzle over the salad and serve.

**Serving suggestion**
Serve with crusty bread as a light, casual summer starter dish.

PREPARATION 10 minutes

COOKING none

SERVES 4

## Cook's tip

You can toast regular pine nuts by tossing them in a frying pan over medium heat without oil for 2–3 minutes, or until golden.

EACH SERVING PROVIDES
1010 kJ, 241 kcal, 15 g protein, 18 g fat (8 g saturated fat), 3 g carbohydrate (3 g sugars), 2 g fibre, 216 mg sodium

# Tomato, cucumber & artichoke salad

PREPARATION 10 minutes

COOKING 10 minutes

SERVES 4

## Shortcut ingredients

Rather than toasting the wraps, sprinkle some ready-made croutons or crisp, broken gourmet crackers over the salad.

EACH SERVING PROVIDES
343 kJ, 82 kcal, 6 g protein, 1 g fat
(<1 g saturated fat), 11 g carbohydrate
(3 g sugars), 4 g fibre, 139 mg sodium

**2 spinach and herb wraps (flat breads)**

**125 g (4 oz) snow peas (mangetout)**

**2 Lebanese or other small cucumbers**

**250 g (8 oz) baby roma (plum) tomatoes**

**250 g (8 oz) marinated artichokes in oil**

1  Preheat the oven to 200°C (400°F/Gas 6). Lightly spray both sides of the spinach wraps with cooking oil spray. Place on a baking tray lined with baking (parchment) paper and bake for 8–10 minutes, or until lightly browned. Allow to cool, then break into bite-sized pieces.

2  Meanwhile, trim the snow peas and cut in half diagonally. Place in a heatproof bowl, cover with boiling water and leave for 1–2 minutes, or until just softened. Drain and refresh under cold running water, then drain again and place in a large salad bowl.

3  Dice the cucumbers, leaving the skin on and removing the seeds if desired; add to the salad bowl. Halve the tomatoes and quarter the artichokes, reserving the artichoke oil, and add to the salad.

4  Add the toasted bread bits to the salad and gently toss together. Drizzle with the reserved artichoke oil and serve immediately.

**Serving suggestion**
Try this salad with chargrilled chicken or steak.

## Variations

- Whisk some lemon juice with the artichoke oil for extra tang.
- Use pita breads or tortillas instead of the wraps.
- Replace the snow peas with blanched asparagus.
- Add watercress sprigs, julienned radish or thin strips of red capsicum (bell pepper).

# Tuna salad with pink grapefruit

500 g (1 lb) fresh tuna or bonito fillets, skinned

2 small pink grapefruit

2 small avocados

2 tablespoons white wine vinegar

100 g (3½ oz) baby rocket (arugula) leaves

PREPARATION 10 minutes

COOKING 10 minutes

SERVES 4

## Shortcut ingredient

Instead of fresh tuna, use smoked trout (or canned tuna in a flavoured oil) and omit step 1.

EACH SERVING PROVIDES
1708 kJ, 408 kcal, 34 g protein, 28 g fat
(7 g saturated fat), 4 g carbohydrate
(4 g sugars), 2 g fibre, 66 mg sodium

1  Heat a frying pan over medium heat. Lightly brush the tuna fillets with olive oil and cook for 2–3 minutes on each side, or until done to your liking. Remove from the pan and leave to cool, then break into large chunks.

2  Meanwhile, cut the top and bottom off each grapefruit. Stand the grapefruit on one cut end on a chopping board. Remove the peel by cutting down around each grapefruit, to the chopping board. Slice or segment the grapefruit by cutting the flesh out in wedges from between the membranes.

3  Cut each avocado in half, twisting to release each one from the central stone. Gently hit the seed with a large knife and twist slightly to release. Using a large spoon, scoop under the flesh to separate it from the skin. Slice the flesh.

4  Whisk the vinegar with ¼ cup (60 ml) extra virgin olive oil and some salt and freshly ground black pepper. Place the tuna, grapefruit, avocado, rocket and dressing in a large salad bowl. Gently toss together and serve.

## Variations

- Replace the pink grapefruit with the sweeter ruby grapefruit, orange segments or diced mango.
- Omit the grapefruit and add tomato wedges and black olives.
- Add fresh mint or coriander (cilantro) leaves.

# Moroccan couscous salad

PREPARATION 10 minutes

COOKING 5 minutes

SERVES 4

## Variations

● Substitute or add slivered almonds, chopped dates and/or dried apricots.

● For a stronger lemon flavour, add grated lemon zest, or finely chopped preserved lemon rind.

● Add pomegranate seeds, fresh coriander (cilantro) or flat-leaf parsley or chopped chilli.

EACH SERVING PROVIDES
1558 kJ, 372 kcal, 13 g protein, 9 g fat
(1 g saturated fat), 60 g carbohydrate
(3 g sugars), 3 g fibre, 10 mg sodium

1½ cups (280 g) instant couscous

½ cup (75 g) currants, or ½ cup (60 g) sultanas (golden raisins)

½ cup (65 g) shelled pistachios

1 tablespoon Moroccan spice mix (see Basics)

2 tablespoons lemon juice

1  Combine the couscous, currants and 1½ cups (375 ml) boiling water in a large bowl. Stir with a fork and leave to soak for 5 minutes, or until all the water is absorbed.

2  Meanwhile, fry the pistachios in a frying pan over medium heat for 3–4 minutes, or until lightly browned, stirring occasionally. Remove from the pan and roughly chop.

3  Fluff the couscous with a fork to break up the lumps. Add the pistachios and sprinkle with the spice mix.

4  Mix the lemon juice with 2 tablespoons extra virgin olive oil, then stir through the couscous. Season to taste with salt and freshly ground black pepper. Serve straight away, or refrigerate until required.

### Serving suggestion
Delicious with lamb cutlets or loin fillets and natural (plain) yogurt.

# Chickpea orange salad with tahini dressing

**400 g (14 oz) broccoli florets**
**420 g (15 oz) can chickpeas**
**2 oranges**
**2 tablespoons tahini**
**¼ teaspoon ground cumin, or to taste**

PREPARATION 10 minutes

COOKING 5 minutes

SERVES 4

## Cook's tip

If the oranges are very sweet, add a squeeze of lemon juice. This salad can be made ahead if required.

EACH SERVING PROVIDES
725 kJ, 173 kcal, 11 g protein, 8 g fat
(1 g saturated fat), 14 g carbohydrate
(6 g sugars), 10 g fibre, 187 mg sodium

1 Cook the broccoli in a saucepan of boiling water (or microwave in a covered container with 1 tablespoon water) for 2–3 minutes, or until just cooked but still firm. Drain and refresh under cold running water, then drain again and allow to cool.

2 Meanwhile, rinse and drain the chickpeas, then place in a salad bowl. Peel one of the oranges, then dice or cut into segments (remove the membranes if segmenting). Add to the chickpeas with the broccoli.

3 Juice the remaining orange. Whisk the orange juice with the tahini, cumin and some salt and freshly ground black pepper, then drizzle over the salad and serve.

## Serving suggestion
Serve with chargrilled chicken, fish or lamb cutlets.

# Thai beef salad

**500 g (1 lb) piece of rump steak**
**3 carrots, about 90 g (3 oz) each**
**1½ tablespoons lime juice**
**3 teaspoons fish sauce**
**4 tablespoons fresh coriander (cilantro) leaves**

1 Heat a frying pan over medium–high heat. Lightly brush the steak with vegetable oil and cook for 2–3 minutes on each side for medium–rare, or until done to your liking. Remove from the pan and set aside to cool. Reserve any pan juices for the dressing.

2 Peel the carrots. Use a food processor or shredder to cut them into thin julienne strips, or peel them into thin ribbons using a vegetable peeler. Place in a large salad bowl.

3 Thinly slice the beef, then add to the carrot.

4 Whisk the lime juice, fish sauce and coriander with any pan juices from the beef. Drizzle over the salad, toss together and serve.

## Variations
- Add 1–2 teaspoons sesame oil to the dressing, or sprinkle the salad with toasted sesame seeds.
- For a bit of heat, add some seeded and finely chopped red chilli.

PREPARATION 10 minutes

COOKING 10 minutes

SERVES 4

## Quick tip
To speed up the cooking time, slice the beef into thin strips, or to reduce the preparation time, buy the beef already cut into strips for stir-frying.

EACH SERVING PROVIDES
716 kJ, 171 kcal, 28 g protein, 6 g fat (2 g saturated fat), 2 g carbohydrate (2 g sugars), 1 g fibre, 412 mg sodium

# Beetroot, rocket & goat's cheese salad

PREPARATION 10 minutes

COOKING none

SERVES 4

## Cook's tip

When handling beetroot, it's a good idea to wear gloves to stop your hands getting stained.

EACH SERVING PROVIDES
945 kJ, 226 kcal, 6 g protein, 19 g fat
(7 g saturated fat), 7 g carbohydrate
(7 g sugars), 3 g fibre, 297 mg sodium

This dramatic salad is very flavoursome. Instead of using goat's cheese you can also use halved bocconcini (fresh baby mozzarella balls) or crumbled fetta in the salad.

**1¾ cups (60 g) wild rocket (arugula)**

**425 g (15 oz) can or bottle of baby beetroot (beets)**

**75 g (2½ oz) goat's cheese**

**1 large ripe avocado**

**3 teaspoons white wine vinegar**

1  Arrange the rocket around a wide, shallow serving bowl.

2  Drain the beetroot well, then cut them into halves or quarters. Dice the avocado.

3  Arrange the beetroot and avocado over the rocket, then crumble the goat's cheese over the top.

4  Whisk the vinegar with 1½ tablespoons extra virgin olive oil and season with salt and freshly ground black pepper. Drizzle over the salad and serve.

## Variation

Try this delicious version with chargrilled fish: substitute the rocket with 400 g (14 oz) lightly blanched green beans, replace the avocado with ⅓ cup (40 g) toasted slivered almonds, and instead of goat's cheese use 175 g (6 oz) fetta marinated in herbs and oil, then toss the salad with 2 tablespoons of the fetta marinating oil whisked with 1 tablespoon lemon juice.

# Smoked chicken, avocado & brie salad

PREPARATION 10 minutes

COOKING none

SERVES 4

## Variations

● Substitute fetta or blue cheese for the brie.
● Add sliced pear or mango.
● Use barbecued chicken, duck or smoked turkey.

EACH SERVING PROVIDES
1698 kJ, 406 kcal, 25 g protein, 32 g fat
(11 g saturated fat), 2 g carbohydrate
(2 g sugars), 1 g fibre, 254 mg sodium

2 smoked chicken breasts, about 150 g (5 oz) each
125 g (4 oz) brie
125 g (4 oz) mesclun or mixed salad greens
1 avocado
¼ cup (60 ml) sushi vinegar

1 Discard the skin from the chicken breasts. Roughly chop or shred the flesh and place in a salad bowl.

2 Slice the brie, then add to the salad bowl with the mesclun.

3 Cut the avocado in half and remove the stone and skin. Slice the flesh and add to the salad bowl with the vinegar. Gently toss together and serve.

**Serving suggestion**
Serve with crusty bread for a decadent lunch or brunch.

# Mixed bean salad

250 g (8 oz) green beans
420 g (15 oz) can mixed beans
250 g (8 oz) baby truss tomatoes
1¾ cups (60 g) baby rocket (arugula) leaves
2 tablespoons Italian dressing

1   Steam, microwave or boil the beans for 2–3 minutes, or until just softened. Drain and refresh under cold running water, then drain again and place in a large salad bowl.

2   Rinse and drain the canned beans, then add to the green beans.

3   Cut the tomatoes in half and add to the salad with the rocket and dressing. Toss together and serve.

## Serving suggestion
This salad is lovely with all kinds of barbecued meats. It also makes a great picnic salad, but toss the dressing through just before serving.

PREPARATION 10 minutes

COOKING 5 minutes

SERVES 4

## Variations
●  Add black olives and diced haloumi or sliced bocconcini (fresh baby mozzarella balls).
●  Add blanched broad (fava) beans, or thinly sliced raw green or yellow zucchini (courgette).

EACH SERVING PROVIDES
458 kJ, 110 kcal, 6 g protein, 4 g fat (<1 g saturated fat), 13 g carbohydrate (4 g sugars), 7 g fibre, 336 mg sodium

salads

# Rice noodle papaya salad

PREPARATION 10 minutes

COOKING none

SERVES 4

EACH SERVING PROVIDES
1416 kJ, 338 kcal, 13 g protein, 6 g fat
(1 g saturated fat), 57 g carbohydrate
(8 g sugars), 3 g fibre, 1536 mg sodium

**200 g (7 oz) dried rice noodles (thick or thin)**

**500 g (1 lb) papaya or mango**

**200 g (7 oz) marinated tofu (with Thai flavourings)**

**⅓ cup (80 ml) sesame ginger soy sauce**

**2 tablespoons chopped fresh coriander (cilantro) or mint**

1  Fill an electric kettle with water and bring to a boil. Place the noodles in a large, heatproof bowl. Cover with boiling water and soak for 5 minutes, or until the noodles have softened. Drain well. Using scissors, snip the noodles into thirds, then place in a large salad bowl.

2  Meanwhile, remove the seeds from the papaya, then peel and dice the flesh. Thinly slice the tofu.

3  Add the papaya, tofu, soy sauce and coriander to the noodles. Toss well and serve.

**Serving suggestion**
Serve with cooked prawns (shrimp), or grilled salmon, beef or chicken.

## Variations

- Use rice vermicelli or glass noodles instead of rice noodles.
- Replace the sesame ginger soy sauce with lime juice, sweet chilli sauce, or a dressing made by mixing 3 tablespoons soy sauce with 1 tablespoon sesame oil.

# Prawn, peach & snow pea salad

**250 g (8 oz) snow peas (mangetout)**

**2 peaches**

**500 g (1 lb) cooked, peeled prawns (shrimp)**

**2 tablespoons lime juice**

**8 cos (romaine) lettuce leaves**

1  Trim the snow peas and cut them in half diagonally. Place in a heatproof bowl, cover with boiling water and leave for 1–2 minutes, or until just softened. Drain and refresh under cold running water, then drain again and place in a large salad bowl.

2  Peel, halve and dice the peaches. Add to the snow peas, along with the prawns.

3  Whisk the lime juice with ¼ cup (60 ml) extra virgin olive oil and some salt and freshly ground black pepper. Pour over the salad and gently mix to combine.

4  Arrange the lettuce leaves on a serving platter. Neatly pile the salad over the top and serve.

## Variations

- Add chopped fresh coriander (cilantro) or mint.
- For extra bite, add a chopped red chilli.
- Roughly tear the cos lettuce and add to the salad.
- Substitute mango or avocado for the peaches, and snow pea sprouts for the snow peas.
- Instead of prawns, use other cooked crustaceans such as crayfish or lobster tails, or a combination.

PREPARATION 10 minutes

COOKING none

SERVES 4

## Cook's tip

If time permits, cook your own raw prawns. Cook them whole in a pot of gently boiling salted water for 3 minutes, or until the flesh turns white. Alternatively, peel and chargrill them.

EACH SERVING PROVIDES
748 kJ, 178 kcal, 28 g protein, 2 g fat (<1 g saturated fat), 10 g carbohydrate (6 g sugars), 3 g fibre, 190 mg sodium

poultry

# Take a barbecued chicken and...

A whole cooked chicken can be transformed into so many tasty meals. Grab one on the way home from work and dinner will be ready in a flash. The delicious aroma will also lure the whole family into the kitchen, eager to help get dinner on the table!

## Summer pasta salad

Bring a full electric kettle of water to a boil, then pour the water into a large saucepan. Cover and place over high heat until boiling. Season the water with a good pinch of salt and add 350 g (12 oz) penne, or other short pasta. Cover and return to a boil, then cook for 10 minutes, or until al dente. Meanwhile, pull the meat from a barbecued chicken and tear it into shreds. Halve 250 g (8 oz) cherry tomatoes and chop 150 g (5 oz) grilled marinated eggplant (aubergine).

Drain the pasta into a colander and rinse under cold running water; drain well. Place in a large serving bowl. Toss ⅓ cup (90 g) pesto through, coating the pasta. Add the chicken, tomatoes and eggplant. Season to taste, gently toss to combine and serve.

## Chicken tacos

Preheat the oven to 180°C (350°F/Gas 4). Lay 12 taco shells on a baking tray and heat for 5 minutes, or according to the packet directions. Meanwhile, pull the meat from a barbecued chicken and tear it into shreds. Mix with 200 ml (7 fl oz) taco sauce. Grate 1 cup (100 g) cheddar and shred ½ iceberg lettuce and place in separate bowls. Serve up all the ingredients for diners to assemble their own tacos.

## Chicken & fetta parcels

Preheat the oven to 200°C (400°F/Gas 6). Pull the meat from a barbecued chicken and chop it. Combine in a bowl with 1 cup (150 g) frozen peas and 100 g (3½ oz) crumbled fetta. Lay out 1 sheet of filo pastry and brush with olive oil. Lay another sheet on top, brush with oil, then lay a third sheet on top. Mound one-quarter of the chicken mixture onto the filo, at one end, about 7 cm (2¾ inches) in from each side. Fold the end over, then the sides, and roll up to enclose. Repeat with more filo sheets and the remaining chicken mixture to make four parcels.

Place the parcels seam side down on a baking tray and brush with olive oil. Sprinkle with 2 teaspoons sesame seeds and bake for 15 minutes, or until they are crisp and golden brown.

## Chicken 'burgers'

Pull the meat from a barbecued chicken and cut into slices. Cut 4 round hamburger buns in half horizontally, then toast until golden brown. Spread the bases with mayonnaise and top with rocket (arugula) leaves and 2 small sliced tomatoes. Top with the chicken and another dollop of mayonnaise. Season to taste, replace the bun top and serve.

## Some quick tips about the chicken

- Barbecued, roast or rotisserie chickens usually come in two sizes — regular or large. The recipes here use meat from a regular-size chicken and serve four people. To strip the meat, simply pull it off with your fingers, picking off as much as you can from the bones. Shred the meat by pulling it apart with your fingers, or chop or slice it as directed. If you want to reduce the fat, remove the skin from the chicken — though it is very flavoursome! You can keep the carcass to make chicken stock.

## Chicken caesar salad

Chop 3 rindless bacon slices (bacon strips) and cut 4 thick slices of day-old bread into 1.5 cm (⅝ inch) cubes. Heat 1 tablespoon olive oil in a large frying pan and cook the bacon over medium heat for 2 minutes. Add the bread and cook, turning occasionally, for 5 minutes, or until crisp and lightly browned. Transfer to a plate lined with paper towels to cool.

Meanwhile, pull the meat from a barbecued chicken and tear it into pieces. Pull the very outer leaves from a cos (romaine) lettuce and discard; tear the inner leaves into large pieces. Combine in a large bowl with the chicken, bacon and croutons. Drizzle with 2–3 tablespoons caesar salad dressing, toss to coat and serve.

## Creamy chicken pasta

Bring a full electric kettle of water to a boil, then pour the water into a large saucepan. Cover and place over high heat until boiling. Season the water with a good pinch of salt and add 350 g (12 oz) pasta spirals. Cover and return to a boil, then cook for 10 minutes, or until al dente. Meanwhile, pull the meat from a barbecued chicken and roughly chop.

Heat 1 tablespoon olive oil in a large deep frying pan. Cook 200 g (7 oz) sliced button mushrooms over medium heat for 3 minutes, or until soft and lightly golden. Add 300 ml (10 fl oz) pouring (light) cream and bring just to a boil. Drain the pasta and add to the frying pan, along with 100 g (3½ oz) baby English spinach leaves. Toss to combine and wilt the spinach, then serve.

## Chicken & sweet corn soup

Pull the meat from a barbecued chicken, remove the skin and finely shred the meat. Finely slice 4 spring onions (scallions) diagonally. Heat 2 teaspoons vegetable oil in a large saucepan and cook the spring onions over medium–low heat for 4 minutes, or until soft. Stir in 2½ cups (625 ml) chicken stock, a 440 g (15 oz) can creamed corn, 1 cup (250 ml) coconut milk and the chicken. Bring to a boil, reduce the heat, simmer for 5 minutes and serve.

## Asian chicken slaw

Pull the meat from a barbecued chicken, tear it into shreds and place in a bowl. Finely shred 300 g (10 oz) cabbage, grate 1 large carrot and toss with the chicken. In a small bowl, mix together ¼ cup (60 ml) each sweet chilli sauce and lime juice. Toss through the salad and serve.

## Chicken melts

Cut 8 thick slices from a country-style loaf. Toast the bread on both sides under a grill (broiler), then cool slightly. Pull the meat from a barbecued chicken and cut into slices. Spread the toasts thickly with avocado and top with the chicken. Arrange 2 sliced tomatoes over the toasts and sprinkle with 1 cup (100 g) grated cheddar. Place the toasts on a baking tray and grill (broil) for 2 minutes, or until the cheese is melted and bubbling. Serve hot.

# Butter chicken

500 g (1 lb) boneless, skinless chicken thighs
420 g (15 oz) jar of Butter Chicken simmer sauce
1 cup (200 g) basmati rice
250 g (8 oz) broccolini
½ cup (15 g) fresh coriander (cilantro) leaves

PREPARATION 10 minutes

COOKING 15 minutes

SERVES 4

1  Fill an electric kettle with water and bring to a boil. Pour the boiling water into a medium saucepan until three-quarters full and bring to a boil over high heat. Rinse the rice under warm running water, stir into the boiling water and boil for 14 minutes, or until tender. Drain.

2  Meanwhile, cut the chicken thighs in half crosswise, then cut each half into 2 cm (¾ inch) chunks, discarding any fat. Place in a saucepan with the simmer sauce and bring to a simmer over medium–high heat, stirring to combine. Reduce the heat to low, then cover and cook for 12 minutes, adding a little water if necessary.

3  While the chicken and rice are cooking, trim the broccolini stalks and cut the broccolini in half crosswise. Cut any thick stalks in half lengthwise. Place in a saucepan and pour in just enough boiling water from the kettle to barely cover. Bring to a boil, then reduce the heat and simmer for 2–3 minutes, or until tender. Drain.

4  Stir half the coriander into the butter chicken. Spoon the rice onto serving plates, top with the chicken and sauce, and arrange the broccolini to the side. Sprinkle the chicken with the remaining coriander and serve.

## Variation

Instead of broccolini, use any green vegetable you like, such as green beans, brussels sprouts or sliced zucchini (courgette).

## Shopping tip

For best results, choose a good-quality simmer sauce — preferably one containing fresh ingredients such as tomatoes, onions, cream, garlic and ginger purée, cardamom and other spices, and coriander (cilantro) and fenugreek leaves.

EACH SERVING PROVIDES
2108 kJ, 504 kcal, 33 g protein, 18 g fat (7 g saturated fat), 55 g carbohydrate (10 g sugars), 1 g fibre, 532 mg sodium

# Hoisin chicken & noodles

PREPARATION 10 minutes

COOKING 15 minutes

SERVES 4

## Shopping tip

For this recipe, buy a packet of fresh mixed vegetables that have been already cut for stir-frying.

## Cook's tip

You can also toss the cooked noodles through the chicken mixture before serving.

EACH SERVING PROVIDES
1946 kJ, 465 kcal, 31 g protein, 17 g fat (4 g saturated fat), 44 g carbohydrate (9 g sugars), 5 g fibre, 494 mg sodium

This quick, tasty recipe is sure to become a family favourite. Now you can enjoy great Chinese any night of the week.

**450 g (15 oz) thick fresh noodles**

**500 g (1 lb) boneless, skinless chicken thighs**

**400 g (14 oz) packet of fresh stir-fry vegetables**

**2½ tablespoons hoisin sauce**

**⅓ cup (50 g) toasted cashews**

1  Fill an electric kettle with water and bring to a boil. Pour the boiling water into a saucepan and return to a boil over high heat. Add the noodles and cook, stirring, for 3 minutes, or until the noodles have separated. Drain.

2  Meanwhile, cut the chicken into 2 cm (¾ inch) cubes. Heat 1 tablespoon vegetable oil in a wok over high heat. Working in two batches, add the chicken and stir-fry for 3 minutes, or until browned and cooked. Transfer to a bowl.

3  Add the vegetables and 2 tablespoons water to the wok and stir-fry for 3 minutes, or until the vegetables are tender. Return the chicken and its juices to the wok, along with the hoisin sauce and cashews. Stir-fry for 2 minutes, or until well combined.

4  Arrange the noodles on a large serving plate. Spoon the chicken and vegetables over the top and serve.

# Tandoori chicken skewers

This dish is great for lazy, impromptu barbecues, or those long summer nights when it's too hot to cook indoors.

**750 g (1½ lb) boneless, skinless chicken breasts**
**4 tablespoons tandoori paste**
**2 tablespoons natural (plain) yogurt**
**4 naan breads**
**½ cup (125 g) tzatziki (see Basics)**

1  Heat a barbecue grill over medium–high heat and brush with vegetable oil. Reduce the heat to medium.

2  Meanwhile, cut the chicken into 2.5 cm (1 inch) cubes. Place in a bowl with the tandoori paste and yogurt and mix to combine. Thread the chicken onto eight 24 cm (9½ inch) metal skewers.

3  Place the skewers on the grill and barbecue them for 8–10 minutes, or until cooked through, turning regularly. Meanwhile, wrap the naan breads in foil and place on the barbecue grill for 2 minutes on each side to warm through.

4  Serve the skewers on the naan breads, drizzled with the tzatziki.

## Serving suggestion
Serve with a simple salad, or even just some mixed salad leaves.

PREPARATION 10 minutes

COOKING 10 minutes

SERVES 4

## Cook's tip
You can also use bamboo instead of metal skewers, but soak them first in water for 10 minutes so they don't burn.

## Shopping tip
Look for tandoori paste in the international section of your supermarket.

EACH SERVING PROVIDES
2515 kJ, 601 kcal, 50 g protein, 25 g fat (10 g saturated fat), 41 g carbohydrate (7 g sugars), 2 g fibre, 1266 mg sodium

poultry

# Crumbed chicken strips

PREPARATION 10 minutes

COOKING 15 minutes

SERVES 4

EACH SERVING PROVIDES
2342 kJ, 559 kcal, 61 g protein, 17 g fat
(5 g saturated fat), 39 g carbohydrate
(4 g sugars), 1 g fibre, 716 mg sodium

**6 cups (180 g) cornflakes**

**2 eggs**

**2 tablespoons dijon mustard**

**2 tablespoons chopped fresh chives**

**4 boneless, skinless chicken breasts, about 250 g (8 oz) each**

1 Preheat the oven to 200°C (400°F/Gas 6). Line a baking tray with baking (parchment) paper. Put the cornflakes in a clean plastic bag and crush into crumbs using a rolling pin.

2 In a bowl, whisk the eggs and mustard until well combined. Stir in the chives and season with salt and freshly ground black pepper.

3 Remove the tenderloins (tenders) from the chicken breasts, then cut the breasts crosswise into slices 1.5 cm (⅝ inch) thick. Dip the chicken pieces and tenderloins into the egg mixture, allowing the excess to run off, then toss to coat in the cornflake crumbs. Place on the baking tray.

4 Bake for 15 minutes, or until the chicken is cooked through and the crumbs are golden brown.

## Serving suggestion
Serve wrapped in a tortilla, with coleslaw or assorted salad items.

# Pasta with chicken meatballs

**400 g (14 oz) dried spaghetti**
**500 g (1 lb) minced (ground) chicken**
**½ cup (40 g) fresh breadcrumbs, made from day-old bread**
**750 g (1½ lb) bottle pasta sauce**
**3 tablespoons fresh basil, torn in half**

1 Fill an electric kettle with water and bring to a boil. Pour the water into a large saucepan and return to a boil. Add the pasta and cook for 10 minutes, or according to the packet instructions, until al dente. Drain.

2 Meanwhile, place the chicken and breadcrumbs in a bowl, season with salt and freshly ground black pepper and mix until well combined. Roll tablespoons of the mixture into balls. Heat 1½ tablespoons olive oil in large non-stick frying pan over medium–high heat. Add the meatballs and cook, turning, for 5 minutes, or until golden brown.

3 Add the pasta sauce to the pan and simmer for 5–6 minutes, or until the meatballs are cooked. Stir in the basil and serve with the pasta.

## Serving suggestion
Serve the pasta sprinkled with shaved or shredded parmesan.

PREPARATION 10 minutes

COOKING 15 minutes

SERVES 4

## Variation
Add chopped fresh parsley and garlic to the meatball mixture.

EACH SERVING PROVIDES
2882 kJ, 688 kcal, 41 g protein, 13 g fat (4 g saturated fat), 99 g carbohydrate (15 g sugars), <1 g fibre, 826 mg sodium

# Turkey patties on baguette

PREPARATION 10 minutes

COOKING 15 minutes

SERVES 4

## Shopping tip

Look for minced turkey in the meat section of supermarkets.

EACH SERVING PROVIDES
2511 kJ, 600 kcal, 52 g protein, 22 g fat
(5 g saturated fat), 47 g carbohydrate
(14 g sugars), 3 g fibre, 770 mg sodium

500 g (1 lb) minced (ground) turkey

2 baguettes, each about 30 cm (12 inches) long

3 tablespoons good-quality whole-egg mayonnaise

8 baby cos (romaine) lettuce leaves

4 tablespoons mango chutney

1  Place the turkey in a bowl and season with salt and freshly ground black pepper. Shape into four sausage-shaped patties, about 12 cm (4½ inches) long and 2 cm (¾ inch) thick.

2  Heat 1 tablespoon olive oil in a large frying pan over medium heat. Add the patties and cook for 7 minutes on each side, or until browned and cooked through.

3  Meanwhile, cut each baguette in half, crosswise through the centre, to make four pieces overall. Slice each portion lengthwise through the middle, without cutting all the way through the bread.

4  Spread the mayonnaise inside each baguette. Fill with the lettuce and patties, dollop the chutney on top and serve.

## Variations
- You can use minced chicken instead of turkey.
- Add chopped fresh parsley or coriander (cilantro) to the patties.

# Quick chicken curry

300 g (10 oz) frozen mixed vegetables (such as
  baby corn, baby grean beans and carrots)
500 g (1 lb) boneless, skinless chicken thighs
2 tablespoons green curry paste
400 ml (14 fl oz) can coconut cream
1 cup (250 ml) chicken stock

1  Set the frozen vegetables out to thaw. Cut the chicken into
2.5 cm (1 inch) cubes.

2  Heat a wok over medium heat, then add the curry paste to the wok
and stir briefly. Add the chicken and stir-fry for 1–2 minutes, tossing
to ensure the paste doesn't burn.

3  Add the coconut cream and stock and bring to a boil, then reduce
the heat to low and simmer for 6 minutes.

4  Stir in the thawed vegetables and simmer for a further 2 minutes,
or until the chicken is cooked. Serve immediately.

## Serving suggestion
Serve with steamed rice, garnished with coriander (cilantro) leaves.

## Variations
•  You can replace the chicken thighs with chicken pieces — you'll just
need to cook them a little longer (about an extra 10 minutes or so).
•  Replace the green curry paste with red curry paste (see our red curry
paste recipe in Basics).

PREPARATION 10 minutes

COOKING 15 minutes

SERVES 4

## Cook's tip
Commercial curry pastes can vary
in heat, so if you don't like your
curries too hot, err on the safe
side and use a little less than
suggested. If a curry is too hot,
adding some fresh lemon or lime
juice will help cool it down.

EACH SERVING PROVIDES
1790 kJ, 427 kcal, 28 g protein, 32 g fat
(21 g saturated fat), 7 g carbohydrate
(6 g sugars), 2 g fibre, 825 mg sodium

# Five-spiced duck salad

PREPARATION 10 minutes

COOKING 15 minutes

SERVES 4

## Shortcut ingredient

Instead of cooking the duck breasts, buy a Chinese barbecued duck, shred the meat and toss it through the salad. You may not need to use quite as much soy sauce to dress the salad.

EACH SERVING PROVIDES
1327 kJ, 317 kcal, 30 g protein, 6 g fat
(2 g saturated fat), 32 g carbohydrate
(2 g sugars), <1 g fibre, 1065 mg sodium

**1 teaspoon Chinese five-spice**

**2½ tablespoons soy sauce**

**4 duck breasts**

**450 g (15 oz) thin hokkien (egg) noodles**

**100 g (3½ oz) packet Asian salad mix**

1  Combine the five-spice and 1 tablespoon of the soy sauce in a small bowl. Brush both sides of each duck breast with the mixture.

2  Heat a large non-stick frying pan over medium–high heat. Add the duck breasts, skin side down, and cook for 6 minutes, or until golden brown and crisp. Turn and cook for a further 4 minutes for medium–rare, or until done to your liking. Transfer to a plate and set aside for 5 minutes to rest. Using a large sharp knife, cut the duck across the grain into thin slices.

3  Meanwhile, fill an electric kettle with water and bring to a boil. Pour the water into a saucepan and return to a boil. Add the noodles and cook for 2 minutes, or until tender. Drain and rinse under cold running water, then drain again.

4  In a large bowl, whisk together the remaining soy and 1 tablespoon peanut oil. Add the drained noodles and toss. Add the salad leaves and duck and toss gently to combine. Serve immediately.

## Variations

● For extra colour and crunch, toss some thinly sliced capsicum (bell pepper) through the salad.
● Replace the duck with chicken.

# Pear, walnut & blue cheese stuffed chicken

**4 boneless, skinless chicken breasts, about 200 g (7 oz) each**
**2 pears**
**¼ cup (30 g) chopped walnuts**
**60 g (2 oz) blue cheese**
**8 slices prosciutto**

1  Preheat the oven to 200°C (400°F/Gas 6). Cut each pear into quarters and remove the cores. Cut six of the pear quarters in half, toss in a bowl with 1 tablespoon olive oil and set aside. Peel the remaining two pear quarters, cut into small cubes and place in a bowl with the walnuts; crumble the cheese over the top and mix together well.

2  Using a small sharp knife, cut a deep pocket into each chicken breast. Evenly divide the pear, cheese and nut mixture among the chicken breasts, then secure the opening with toothpicks. Wrap two prosciutto slices around each chicken breast.

3  Heat 1 tablespoon olive oil in a large non-stick frying pan that can be transferred to the oven. Add the chicken breasts and cook over medium–high heat for 2 minutes on each side, or until golden brown.

4  Scatter the remaining pear wedges around the frying pan, over the chicken. Transfer the frying pan to the oven and bake the chicken for 10 minutes, or until cooked through. Remove the toothpicks and serve.

## Serving suggestion
Serve with steamed asparagus spears, or a salad of baby spinach.

PREPARATION 10 minutes

COOKING 15 minutes

SERVES 4

## Cook's tip
If possible, use a frying pan that has an ovenproof handle so that it can be transferred to the oven. Alternatively, you can place the chicken breasts on a baking tray. Heat the baking tray in the oven while the oven is heating up.

EACH SERVING PROVIDES
2045 kJ, 489 kcal, 54 g protein, 25 g fat (9 g saturated fat), 12 g carbohydrate (9 g sugars), 3 g fibre, 608 mg sodium

# Balsamic vinegar chicken wings

**1 kg (2 lb) chicken wings**

**2 cloves garlic**

**2½ tablespoons balsamic vinegar**

**2 tablespoons honey**

**1½ tablespoons fresh thyme**

PREPARATION 10 minutes

COOKING 15 minutes

SERVES 4

1   Preheat the oven to 210°C (415°F/Gas 6–7). Line a baking tray with baking (parchment) paper. Cut off and discard the tip of each chicken wing, then cut each wing in half at the joint.

2   Chop the garlic and place in a bowl with the vinegar, honey, 1 tablespoon of the thyme and 2 tablespoons olive oil. Season with salt and freshly ground black pepper and mix until well combined. Add the chicken wings and toss until well coated.

3   Heat 1 tablespoon olive oil in a frying pan over medium heat. Remove the chicken wings from the marinade, add them to the pan and cook, turning, for 10 minutes, or until golden brown.

4   Add the marinade to the pan, partially cover with a lid and cook for a further 3–4 minutes, or until the marinade has thickened into a glaze and the chicken is cooked through. Scatter with the remaining thyme and serve.

## Variation
Replace the thyme with rosemary.

## Cook's tip
The chicken wings can be left to marinate in the fridge for several hours or overnight before cooking. Instead of frying them, you can also bake the wings in a 210°C (415°F/Gas 6–7) oven for 25 minutes, until golden and caramelised.

EACH SERVING PROVIDES
1590 kJ, 380 kcal, 52 g protein, 12 g fat (4 g saturated fat), 14 g carbohydrate (14 g sugars), <1 g fibre, 204 mg sodium

poultry

# Honey mustard glazed chicken

PREPARATION 10 minutes

COOKING 15 minutes

SERVES 4

## Shortcut ingredient

Buy about 12 chicken tenderloins (tenders) instead of the chicken breasts. Fry them for 3 minutes on each side, or until cooked and golden brown, then return them to the pan and coat them in the sauce.

EACH SERVING PROVIDES
1534 kJ, 366 kcal, 44 g protein, 18 g fat
(8 g saturated fat), 8 g carbohydrate
(7 g sugars), <1 g fibre, 131 mg sodium

4 boneless, skinless chicken breasts, about 200 g (7 oz) each
1 tablespoon wholegrain mustard
1 tablespoon honey
½ cup (125 ml) pouring (light) cream
1 tablespoon chopped fresh parsley

1　Season the chicken breasts with a little salt and freshly ground black pepper.

2　Heat 1 tablespoon olive oil in a large non-stick frying pan over medium–high heat. Add the chicken breasts and cook for 7 minutes, then turn and cook the other side for 6 minutes, or until cooked through and golden brown. Transfer the chicken to a plate and cover lightly with foil to keep warm.

3　Reduce the heat to medium. Add the mustard, honey and cream to the pan and cook, stirring, for 1 minute. Stir in the parsley and season to taste.

4　Return the cooked chicken to the pan and turn to coat in the sauce. Serve the chicken immediately, drizzled with the sauce.

**Serving suggestion**
Superb with a sweet potato mash and steamed sugarsnap peas.

## Variation

Omit the cream and parsley, and combine the mustard and honey with the zest and juice of 1 lime, and 1–2 crushed garlic cloves if desired. Spread the mixture over the top of four small chicken breasts (about 125 g/4 oz each). Place on a baking tray lined with baking (parchment) paper and cook under a medium–hot grill (broiler) for 4–5 minutes on each side, or until cooked through.

# Chicken tagine with couscous

Most tagines require lengthy cooking and many ingredients. This super-quick version is very easy and delicious.

**750 g (1½ lb) boneless, skinless chicken thighs**
**3 tablespoons Moroccan spice mix (see Basics)**
**½ cup (75 g) currants**
**2 cups (370 g) instant couscous**

1   Fill an electric kettle with water and bring to a boil. Meanwhile, cut the chicken thighs in half crosswise, then cut each half into strips about 2 cm (¾ inch) wide, discarding any fat. Toss in a bowl with the spice mix, coating well.

2   Heat 1 tablespoon olive oil in a large saucepan over high heat and add the chicken in two batches. Toss for 2 minutes, then return all the chicken to the pan, add 2 cups (500 ml) of the boiling water and mix well. Bring to a boil, then reduce the heat to medium. Stir in the currants, cover and simmer for 10 minutes, or until the chicken is cooked through. Season to taste with salt and freshly ground black pepper.

3   Meanwhile, pour 2 cups (500 ml) of the boiling water into another saucepan and bring to a boil. Remove from the heat and stir in the couscous. Cover and leave to soak for 5 minutes, or until all the water has been absorbed.

4   Fluff the couscous with a fork, breaking up any lumps. Drizzle with 1 tablespoon olive oil and season to taste. Toss again with the fork, then spoon onto serving plates. Top with the tagine mixture and serve.

## Serving suggestion
Steamed green beans are a wonderful accompaniment to this tagine.

PREPARATION 10 minutes

COOKING 15 minutes

SERVES 4

## Cook's tip
A tagine is a Moroccan stew that takes its name from the heavy clay pot in which it is traditionally cooked. The pot has a round flat base and a domed lid that traps the steam during cooking. You don't need a special cooking pot to make a tagine — just use a pot that has a tight-fitting lid, and preferably a heavy base.

EACH SERVING PROVIDES
2631 kJ, 628 kcal, 47 g protein, 15 g fat (4 g saturated fat), 77 g carbohydrate (1 g sugars), 2 g fibre, 180 mg sodium

# Chicken, tomato & fetta salad

PREPARATION 10 minutes

COOKING 15 minutes

SERVES 4

EACH SERVING PROVIDES
1927 kJ, 460 kcal, 49 g protein, 28 g fat
(10 g saturated fat), 2 g carbohydrate
(2 g sugars), 1 g fibre, 500 mg sodium

**4 boneless, skinless chicken breasts, about 200 g (7 oz) each**

**250 g (8 oz) cherry tomatoes (use a mix of different colours, shapes and sizes if desired)**

**2 tablespoons lemon juice**

**230 g (8 oz) jar marinated fetta in oil**

**½ cup (15 g) small basil leaves**

1  Slice the chicken breasts in half lengthwise, then cut in half crosswise. Heat 1 tablespoon olive oil in a non-stick frying pan over medium–high heat. Working in two batches, fry the chicken for 3 minutes on each side, or until golden brown and cooked through. Transfer to a serving plate.

2  Cut the tomatoes in half. Add them to the pan and cook for 2 minutes, or until softened slightly. Add half the lemon juice and toss gently, then scatter the tomatoes over the chicken.

3  Drain the fetta from the oil, reserving 2 tablespoons of the oil. Scatter the fetta over the chicken, along with the basil.

4  Whisk the reserved oil with the remaining lemon juice. Season with salt and freshly ground black pepper and drizzle over the salad.

**Serving suggestion**
Serve this salad with plenty of fresh, crusty bread.

## Variation
You could add some sliced avocado to the salad just before serving.

# Grilled quail with lemon chive butter

PREPARATION 10 minutes

COOKING 15 minutes

SERVES 4

## Shortcut ingredient

To save preparation time, ask your butcher to 'butterfly' or 'spatchcock' the quail for you, or buy quail that have already been opened out.

EACH SERVING PROVIDES
1749 kJ, 418 kcal, 37 g protein, 30 g fat (11 g saturated fat), 1 g carbohydrate (<1 g sugars), <1 g fibre, 159 mg sodium

**4 large quail**

**2 teaspoons ground cumin**

**2 tablespoons butter**

**1 tablespoon lemon juice**

**1½ tablespoons chopped fresh chives**

1   Using kitchen scissors, cut down both sides of the backbone of each quail. Remove and discard the backbone (this makes it easier and quicker to cook the quail). Press down gently on each quail with the palm of your hand to flatten it out slightly. Rub the cumin over both sides of each quail.

2   Heat 1½ tablespoons olive oil in a large non-stick frying pan over medium heat. Place all the quail in the pan, breast side down, and cook for 6 minutes on each side.

3   Add the butter to the pan and allow to melt, then spoon the melted butter over the quail. Add the lemon juice to the pan and season the butter mixture with salt and freshly ground black pepper.

4   Scatter the chives over the quail. Turn each quail over to coat in the lemon chive butter mixture. Serve immediately, drizzled with the lemon chive butter mixture.

### Serving suggestion

Serve on a bed of couscous, with steamed green baby beans or a shaved cucumber and radish salad.

# Chicken & leek sauté

**500 g (1 lb) boneless, skinless chicken breasts**
**1 leek, about 250 g (8 oz)**
**12 asparagus spears**
**2 cloves garlic**
**⅓ cup (80 ml) chicken stock**

1   Slice the chicken breasts crosswise into strips 1 cm (½ inch) wide. Trim the root and green leafy ends from the leek, leaving only the white stem. Wash the stem well to remove any sand or grit, then thinly slice or shred it. Trim the asparagus and cut into 4 cm (1½ inch) lengths.

2   Heat 1½ tablespoons olive oil in a large non-stick frying pan over medium–high heat. Add the chicken in two batches, cooking for 1 minute on each side to seal. Transfer to a plate.

3   Heat another 2 teaspoons oil in the pan. Add the leek and cook, stirring, for 2 minutes, or until slightly softened. Crush the garlic; add to the pan with the asparagus and stock and bring to a simmer.

4   Stir in the chicken, then cover and cook over medium–low heat for 4 minutes, or until the chicken is just cooked through. Season well with salt and freshly ground black pepper and serve.

**Serving suggestion**
Serve the sauté tossed through or on top of hot cooked pasta.

## Variations

• For a citrus tang, squeeze some fresh lemon juice over the dish just before serving.
• Add 1 chopped red chilli with the garlic if you'd like it spicy.
• Use sliced pork fillet instead of chicken.

PREPARATION 10 minutes

COOKING 10 minutes

SERVES 4

## Shortcut ingredient

To make this dish even quicker to prepare, buy some chicken that has already been cut for stir-frying, which will save you having to slice it yourself.

EACH SERVING PROVIDES
831 kJ, 199 kcal, 30 g protein, 7 g fat (2 g saturated fat), 4 g carbohydrate (3 g sugars), 3 g fibre, 190 mg sodium

poultry

# Chicken pizzas

PREPARATION 10 minutes

COOKING 15 minutes

SERVES 4

## Variations

- Add chargrilled capsicum (bell pepper) strips to the pizzas.
- Replace the sun-dried tomato pesto with basil pesto.

EACH SERVING PROVIDES
2892 kJ, 691 kcal, 41 g protein, 27 g fat
(9 g saturated fat), 70 g carbohydrate
(11 g sugars), 6 g fibre, 1411 mg sodium

**2 x 30 cm (12 inch) pizza bases (crusts)**
**½ cup (125 g) ready-made sun-dried tomato pesto**
**½ barbecued chicken**
**225 g (8 oz) bocconcini (fresh baby mozzarella balls)**
**½ cup (15 g) small basil leaves**

1 Preheat the oven to 220°C (425°F/Gas7). Place the pizza bases on two baking trays. Spread the bases evenly with the pesto.

2 Discard the skin and bones from the chicken; slice the flesh and scatter over the pizza bases. Slice the bocconcini and arrange over the pizzas.

3 Bake for 10–12 minutes, or until the pizza crusts are golden brown. Scatter with the basil, cut into wedges and serve.

# Chicken wraps

1 red onion

1 red capsicum (bell pepper)

500 g (1 lb) boneless, skinless chicken breasts

8 x 20 cm (8 inch) flour tortillas

35 g (1 oz) packet taco or burrito seasoning

1  Preheat the oven to 180°C (350°F/Gas 4). Cut the onion into wedges, and the capsicum and chicken into strips.

2  Wrap the tortillas in foil and bake for 10 minutes, or until warmed through. Meanwhile, heat 1 tablespoon olive oil in a large non-stick frying pan over medium heat. Add the onion and capsicum and cook, stirring, for 4 minutes, or until softened. Transfer to a plate.

3  Heat another tablespoon oil in the pan over medium–high heat. Toss the chicken in the seasoning mix, then cook, stirring, for 4 minutes, or until golden brown. Return the capsicum and onion to the pan, along with ⅓ cup (80 ml) water, and cook for 1 minute.

4  Spoon the chicken mixture into the warm wraps. Roll the wraps up, enclosing the filling, and serve immediately.

PREPARATION 10 minutes

COOKING 15 minutes

SERVES 4

## Variation

Add other ingredients to the wraps, such as shredded lettuce, sliced avocado, grated cheese and chopped tomato and coriander (cilantro).

EACH SERVING PROVIDES
1733 kJ, 414 kcal, 34 g protein, 12 g fat (3 g saturated fat), 42 g carbohydrate (6 g sugars), 3 g fibre, 1377 mg sodium

poultry

# Pan-fried lime & coriander chicken strips

PREPARATION 10 minutes

COOKING 15 minutes

SERVES 4

EACH SERVING PROVIDES
1420 kJ, 339 kcal, 45 g protein, 17 g fat
(5 g saturated fat), 2 g carbohydrate
(<1 g sugars), 1 g fibre, 215 mg sodium

**1 lime**

**2 tablespoons chopped fresh coriander (cilantro)**

**2 cloves garlic**

**1 red birdseye (Thai) chilli**

**16 chicken tenderloins (tenders)**

1   Finely grate the zest of the lime, then juice the lime. Put 1 teaspoon lime zest and 2 tablespoons juice in a bowl with the coriander and 2 tablespoons peanut oil.

2   Crush the garlic and finely chop the chilli; add to the bowl with the chicken. Season with salt and freshly ground black pepper and mix well.

3   Heat a non-stick frying pan over medium–high heat. Add half the chicken and fry for 3 minutes on each side, or until cooked and golden brown. Transfer to a plate and cover loosely with foil to keep warm while cooking the remaining chicken. Serve hot.

## Serving suggestion
Serve with cooked rice and your choice of steamed greens.

# Chicken & choy sum stir-fry with rice

PREPARATION 10 minutes

COOKING 15 minutes

SERVES 4

## Cook's tip

If you cook rice regularly, consider using a rice cooker. With these handy appliances you'll never end up with gluggy or overcooked rice, and you won't need to keep an eye on the rice while it's cooking. Once the rice is cooked, many rice cookers also keep the rice warm, ready to serve up whenever the rest of the meal is ready.

EACH SERVING PROVIDES
1808 kJ, 432 kcal, 29 g protein, 10 g fat
(3 g saturated fat), 56 g carbohydrate
(3 g sugars), 2 g fibre, 587 mg sodium

1⅓ cups (265 g) long-grain white rice

500 g (1 lb) boneless, skinless chicken thighs

400 g (14 oz) bunch choy sum (Chinese flowering cabbage)

3 cloves garlic

2 tablespoons oyster sauce

1   Fill an electric kettle with water and bring to a boil. Pour the boiling water into a medium saucepan until three-quarters full and bring to a boil over high heat. Rinse the rice under warm running water, then stir into the boiling water and boil for 14 minutes, or until tender. Drain.

2   Meanwhile, cut the chicken into 2.5 cm (1 inch) cubes, and the choy sum into 5 cm (2 inch) lengths. Heat 1 tablespoon vegetable oil in a wok over high heat. Working in two batches, add the chicken and stir-fry for 3 minutes, or until browned and cooked. Transfer to a bowl.

3   Add the choy sum stems to the wok along with 2 tablespoons water and stir-fry for 2 minutes, or until the choy sum has softened slightly and the water has evaporated. Meanwhile, finely chop the garlic, then add to the wok and stir-fry for 1 minute.

4   Return the chicken to the wok. Add the choy sum leaves and oyster sauce and stir-fry for 1 minute, or until the choy sum leaves have wilted and the mixture is well combined. Serve with the rice.

## Variations

- Replace the chicken with thin strips of beef.
- Add some chopped fresh chilli with the garlic.

# Chicken parmigiana

**4 chicken schnitzels**

**500 g (1 lb) jar tomato pasta sauce**

**2–3 tablespoons fresh basil leaves, torn**

**¾ cup (90 g) grated cheddar cheese**

**100 g (3½ oz) packet salad leaves**

1 Preheat the grill (broiler) to medium. Heat 2 cm (¾ inch) oil in a frying pan over medium–high heat. Working in two batches, cook the chicken for 3 minutes on each side, or until cooked through. Drain on paper towels.

2 Meanwhile, heat the pasta sauce in a saucepan over medium–high heat until it just comes to a boil.

3 Spoon half the pasta sauce over the base of a large ovenproof dish. Arrange the chicken over the sauce, then spoon the remaining sauce over the top. Scatter the basil over and sprinkle with the cheese.

4 Grill (broil) for 2 minutes, or until the cheese has melted and is golden brown. Serve with the salad leaves.

**Serving suggestion**
Dress the salad leaves with a simple vinaigrette (see Basics).

PREPARATION 10 minutes

COOKING 15 minutes

SERVES 4

## Shopping tip
Buy ready-made chicken schnitzels for this recipe.

## Cook's tip
For extra flavour, use a pasta sauce that contains chargrilled vegetables.

EACH SERVING PROVIDES
2841 kJ, 679 kcal, 48 g protein, 33 g fat (12 g saturated fat), 47 g carbohydrate (12 g sugars), 4 g fibre, 1375 mg sodium

meat

# 5 ways with 5 ingredients

Using the five simple ingredients below, you can whip up five deliciously different meals. How clever is that!

## Ingredients

500 g (1 lb) minced (ground) beef
1 finely chopped onion
2 cloves garlic, crushed
410 g (15 oz) can chopped tomatoes
1 cup (60 g) fresh breadcrumbs

## Home-style bake

Preheat the oven to 200°C (400°F/Gas 6). Heat 1 tablespoon olive oil in a frying pan and cook the beef, onion and garlic over high heat for 5 minutes, breaking up any lumps with a wooden spoon. Stir in the tomatoes and season to taste. Transfer to a 20 cm (8 inch) ovenproof dish and sprinkle with the breadcrumbs.

Bake for 10 minutes, or until the breadcrumbs are crisp and golden brown.

**SERVING SUGGESTION** Serve with steamed rice and peas.

## Garlicky kofta skewers

Preheat a barbecue or chargrill pan to medium–high. Using your hands, mix the beef, garlic, breadcrumbs and half the onion until well combined. Divide into eight equal portions, form into sausage shapes about 10 cm (4 inches) long, then press them around eight 20 cm (8 inch) skewers. Cook for 10 minutes, turning occasionally, until well browned and cooked through.

Meanwhile, heat 1 tablespoon olive oil in a small saucepan and cook the remaining onion over medium heat for 5 minutes, or until soft and lightly coloured. Add the tomatoes, bring to a boil, reduce the heat and simmer for 5 minutes. Season to taste, then serve over the skewers.

**SERVING SUGGESTION** Enjoy with a Greek-style salad.

## Sizzling meatballs in rich tomato sauce

Using your hands, mix the beef, breadcrumbs and half the onion and garlic until evenly combined. Roll level tablespoons of the mixture into balls. Heat 1 tablespoon olive oil in a large deep frying pan over medium–high heat.

Add the meatballs and the remaining onion and garlic and cook for 5 minutes, shaking the pan occasionally to turn the meatballs. Stir in the tomatoes and ½ cup (125 ml) water and bring to a boil. Reduce the heat slightly and simmer for 10 minutes, or until the meatballs are cooked through. Season to taste and serve.

**SERVING SUGGESTION** Serve over hot pasta, sprinkled with grated parmesan.

## Low-fat mini meatloaves

Preheat the oven to 200°C (400°F/Gas 6) and lightly grease eight ⅓ cup (80 ml) muffin tin holes. Using your hands, mix the beef (use low-fat mince), breadcrumbs and half the onion and garlic until evenly combined. Divide the mixture into eight equal portions, then press into the muffin holes. Brush the tops with oil and bake for 15 minutes.

Meanwhile, heat 1 tablespoon olive oil in a small saucepan and cook the remaining onion and garlic over medium heat for 5 minutes, or until soft and lightly coloured. Add the tomatoes and bring to a boil. Reduce the heat and simmer for 5 minutes, then season to taste and serve with the meatloaves.

**SERVING SUGGESTION** Great with mashed potatoes and steamed green vegetables.

## Burgers

Lightly oil a frying pan, barbecue or chargrill and preheat to medium–high. Using your hands, mix the beef, breadcrumbs and half the onion and garlic until evenly combined. Divide the mixture into four equal portions, then shape into four round patties, about 10 cm (4 inches) in diameter and 1.5 cm (⅝ inch) thick (they'll shrink during cooking). Cook the burgers for 5 minutes on each side.

Meanwhile, heat 1 tablespoon olive oil in a small saucepan and cook the remaining onion and garlic over medium heat for 5 minutes, or until soft and lightly coloured. Add the tomatoes and bring to a boil, then reduce the heat and simmer for 5 minutes. Season to taste and serve with the burgers.

**SERVING SUGGESTION** Delicious on toasted Turkish bread or ciabatta, with some salad.

# Super-easy steak diane

**PREPARATION** 10 minutes

**COOKING** 15 minutes

**SERVES** 4

## Cook's tip

It takes a little longer, but it's best to cook the steak in two batches, so the steaks brown well and develop good flavour. If you cook them all together they will stew rather than brown.

EACH SERVING PROVIDES
2207 kJ, 527 kcal, 44 g protein, 37 g fat
(23 g saturated fat), 4 g carbohydrate
(3 g sugars), <1 g fibre, 228 mg sodium

For a more traditional steak diane, add a splash of brandy and worcestershire sauce along with the cream in step 3, or add 2–3 tablespoons white wine or sherry instead.

**3 large cloves garlic**

**3 tablespoons butter**

**4 x 200 g (7 oz) beef fillet or boneless beef rib eye steaks (scotch fillets)**

**2 tablespoons chopped fresh flat-leaf parsley**

**300 ml (10 fl oz) pouring (light) cream**

1  Finely chop the garlic and set aside.

2  Heat the butter and 2 tablespoons olive oil in a large frying pan over medium–high heat until the butter is foaming. Working in two batches to avoid overcrowding the pan, cook the steaks for 2 minutes on each side, removing each batch to a plate. Cover loosely with foil to keep warm.

3  Add the garlic to the pan and cook, stirring, until it just begins to colour. Stir in the cream using a wooden spoon or heatproof spatula, scraping all the pan sediment into the cream. Reduce the heat to low and simmer, uncovered, for 4 minutes, or until the mixture is slightly thickened.

4  Stir the parsley into the sauce. Return the steaks to the frying pan and cook for 2 minutes, or until heated through. Serve hot.

**Serving suggestion**
Serve with crispy French fries and a leafy green salad.

meat

# Chargrilled beef patties in lettuce cups

1 iceberg lettuce
500 g (1 lb) minced (ground) beef
4 spring onions (scallions)
2 large limes
⅓ cup (80 ml) soy sauce

PREPARATION 10 minutes

COOKING 10 minutes

SERVES 4

## Quick tip
To make meat patties cook more quickly, make a hole in the middle after you've shaped them. As you cook them, the hole will disappear, as if by magic.

EACH SERVING PROVIDES
958 kJ, 229 kcal, 28 g protein, 12 g fat (5 g saturated fat), 6 g carbohydrate (2 g sugars), 4 g fibre, 1467 mg sodium

1   Using a small sharp knife, remove the core of the lettuce, run cold tap water into the cavity, then turn it upside down to drain. Wrap the lettuce in paper towels and chill in the fridge for 8 minutes.

2   Meanwhile, place the beef in a bowl. Finely chop the spring onions; reserve 2 teaspoons and add the remainder to the beef. Season the beef with salt and freshly ground black pepper and mix well, using your hands to bring the mixture together. Shape the mixture into 16 small, evenly sized balls, then gently flatten them into patties. Brush the patties on both sides with peanut or vegetable oil.

3   Preheat a large chargrill pan or barbecue grill to high. Add the patties, reduce the heat to medium and cook for 4 minutes on each side, or until cooked through, turning them once only. (If using a chargrill pan, you may need to cook them in two batches.)

4   While the patties are cooking, finely grate the zest from the limes, then juice the limes. Combine the lime zest and juice in a small bowl with the soy sauce and reserved spring onions. Gently separate the lettuce leaves into cups, trimming them with scissors if they're large.

5   Serve the patties in the lettuce cups, drizzled with the lime dressing.

### Serving suggestion
Serve with a quick stir-fry of shredded carrot and snow peas (mangetout).

## Variations
- Garnish with shredded red chilli.
- Instead of patties, stir-fry beef strips and serve in the lettuce cups.
- In place of an iceberg lettuce, use two butter leaf lettuces.

# Stir-fried beef with mandarin & bok choy

500 g (1 lb) beef rump steak

2 teaspoons grated fresh ginger

¼ cup (60 ml) hoisin sauce

2 large mandarins (satsumas or clementines)

500 g (1 lb) baby bok choy

PREPARATION 10 minutes

COOKING 10 minutes

SERVES 4

## Cook's tip

Young, new-season ginger has a milder flavour than older ginger. To tell them apart, break a piece at a joint end: the larger the fibre, the older the ginger, and the more pungent it will be.

EACH SERVING PROVIDES
914 kJ, 218 kcal, 28 g protein, 7 g fat (3 g saturated fat), 11 g carbohydrate (10 g sugars), 3 g fibre, 313 mg sodium

1  Cut the beef across the grain into thin strips and place in a bowl. Add the ginger and 2 tablespoons of the hoisin sauce. Mix well, then set the beef aside to marinate for 5 minutes.

2  Meanwhile, cut the mandarins in half across the middle and juice them, reserving ½ cup (125 ml) of the juice. Remove the peel from the mandarins, scrape away the white pith and cut it into very fine shreds. Wash the bok choy and cut any large pieces in half.

3  Heat a wok or large frying pan over high heat. Add 3 teaspoons peanut or vegetable oil and swirl to coat. Working in two batches, stir-fry the beef for 3 minutes, or until well browned and just cooked through, reheating the wok in between. Remove each batch to a plate.

4  Reheat the wok and add another 3 teaspoons oil. Add the shredded mandarin peel and bok choy and stir-fry for 1–2 minutes. Add the mandarin juice and remaining hoisin sauce, then return the beef to the wok and toss to warm through. Serve immediately.

## Serving suggestion
Serve with hot rice noodles tossed with sesame oil and soy sauce.

## Variations
- Replace the mandarin peel and juice with orange zest and juice.
- Use sliced pork, chicken or peeled prawns (shrimp) instead of beef.
- If you don't have hoisin sauce, oyster sauce is equally delicious.

# Chilli con carne

**PREPARATION** 10 minutes

**COOKING** 15 minutes

**SERVES** 4

## Variation

Spoon the mixture in taco shells and top with shredded lettuce, grated cheddar and avocado.

## Cook's tip

If you're out of taco seasoning, use 1 tablespoon ground cumin and 1 teaspoon mild chilli powder.

EACH SERVING PROVIDES
1435 kJ, 342 kcal, 31 g protein, 12 g fat
(5 g saturated fat), 25 g carbohydrate
(14 g sugars), 9 g fibre, 1950 mg sodium

1 large onion

500 g (1 lb) minced (ground) beef

35 g (1 oz) sachet taco seasoning mix

750 g (1½ lb) jar of tomato passata (puréed tomatoes)

420 g (15 oz) can red kidney beans

1  Peel and dice the onion. Meanwhile, heat 1 tablespoon olive oil in a large, deep frying pan over medium–high heat. Add the onion to the pan and cook for 2 minutes, or until softened. Add the beef and cook for a further 2–3 minutes, or until it browns, breaking up the lumps with a wooden spoon.

2  Reduce the heat to medium. Add the taco seasoning mix and stir for 30 seconds. Stir in the tomato passata and mix well.

3  Reduce the heat to medium–low and simmer, uncovered, for 5 minutes. Meanwhile, drain and rinse the beans. Add them to the pan and cook for a further 3 minutes, or until heated through. Serve hot.

### Serving suggestion

Serve with steamed rice, or potatoes baked in their skins — perhaps with a dollop of sour cream or Greek-style yogurt.

# Steak with capsicum & caper relish

4 sirloin (porterhouse) or boneless rib eye steaks (scotch fillets), about 225 g (8 oz) each

2 tablespoons capers

270 g (9½ oz) jar chargrilled capsicum (bell pepper) strips

¼ cup (60 ml) red wine vinegar, plus extra for drizzling

150 g (5 oz) mixed salad leaves or baby rocket (arugula)

1  Brush the steaks lightly with olive oil and season well with salt and freshly ground black pepper. Chop the capers, then combine in a small bowl with the capsicum strips, some oil from the jar and the vinegar.

2  Preheat a barbecue flatplate or chargrill plate to high. Add the steaks and cook, without turning, for 3–4 minutes, or until small beads of moisture appear on top. Turn the steaks and continue to cook until done to your liking. Remove the steaks from the heat and leave to rest for 4 minutes.

3  Meanwhile, put the salad leaves in a bowl, drizzle lightly with some extra virgin olive oil and extra red wine vinegar and toss.

4  Top the steaks with a spoonful of the capsicum and caper relish and serve with the salad leaves.

**Serving suggestion**
Serve with small steamed buttered potatoes and a green salad.

PREPARATION 5 minutes

COOKING 10 minutes

SERVES 4

## Variation
Slice the cooked steaks and toss with the capsicum, capers and salad leaves. Top with slices of pan-fried haloumi cheese.

## Cook's tip
When pressed with tongs, a medium-rare steak will feel soft, yet slightly springy; medium will feel firm; and well-done very firm.

EACH SERVING PROVIDES
1494 kJ, 357 kcal, 47 g protein, 17 g fat (6 g saturated fat), 4 g carbohydrate (2 g sugars), <1 g fibre, 338 mg sodium

meat

145

# Massaman-style beef curry

PREPARATION 10 minutes

COOKING 15 minutes

SERVES 4

## Shortcut ingredients

Relishes, chutneys and curry pastes are great pantry staples. Curry pastes make it very easy to get a quick and tasty curry on the table, while relishes and chutneys add instant zest to plain dishes — try chargrilled meats or skewers with a spoonful of mango chutney and lime pickle.

EACH SERVING PROVIDES
1870 kJ, 447 kcal, 31 g protein, 29 g fat (21 g saturated fat), 15 g carbohydrate (4 g sugars), 3 g fibre, 600 mg sodium

500 g (1 lb) beef rump
2 large potatoes
2–3 tablespoons massaman curry paste
400 ml (14 fl oz) can coconut milk
roasted peanuts, for sprinkling

1 Cut the beef across the grain into thin strips. Peel and cut the potatoes into 1.5 cm (⅝ inch) cubes.

2 Heat a wok or large frying pan over high heat. Add 1 tablespoon peanut or vegetable oil and swirl to coat. Working in two batches, stir-fry the beef for 3 minutes, or until well browned and just cooked through, reheating the wok in between. Remove each batch to a plate.

3 Reheat the wok and add another 1 tablespoon oil. Reduce the heat to low, add the curry paste and cook, stirring, for 1–2 minutes. Stir in the coconut milk and 1 cup (250 ml) water. Increase the heat to medium, add the potatoes and simmer for 5 minutes, or until the potatoes are just tender and the sauce has thickened slightly.

4 Return the beef to the wok and simmer for 1 minute to heat through — do not boil. Season to taste with salt and freshly ground black pepper and serve sprinkled with peanuts.

### Serving suggestion
This curry is wonderful with steamed jasmine rice (Thai fragrant rice).

## Variations
- Sprinkle the finished curry with basil leaves.
- Diced pork fillet is also good in this delicious curry.
- Replace the massaman curry paste with 1–2 tablespoons Thai red or green curry paste, or an Indian-style curry paste like rogan josh.

meat

# Steaks with prosciutto & tomato

PREPARATION 10 minutes

COOKING 10 minutes

SERVES 4

## Cook's tip

You can use a can of peeled tomatoes instead of the pasta sauce. Use scissors to 'chop' the tomatoes in the can, working through the tomatoes several times to make sure they are well chopped.

EACH SERVING PROVIDES
1325 kJ, 317 kcal, 55 g protein, 7 g fat
(3 g saturated fat), 7 g carbohydrate
(6 g sugars), 2 g fibre, 829 mg sodium

Bottled Italian-style tomato pasta sauces are a great standby. Good with pasta, they can also transform a simple steak into a special meal. Try the olive and the basil varieties too.

**8 small veal steaks (or small, thin beef steaks), about 100 g (3½ oz) each**
**8 large basil leaves**
**8 slices prosciutto**
**¼ cup (60 ml) white wine or chicken stock**
**410 g (15 oz) jar of tomato pasta sauce**

1  Lay the steaks on a clean chopping board; top each with a basil leaf, then a prosciutto slice. Use a few toothpicks or a small wooden skewer to secure the prosciutto and basil to the meat. Brush each side of the steaks with a little olive oil.

2  Heat a large non-stick frying pan over medium–high heat. Cook the steaks, in two batches if required, for 2 minutes on each side, or until cooked through. Remove and set aside to rest in a warm place.

3  Add the wine to the pan, let it cook for 30 seconds, then add the tomato pasta sauce. Bring the mixture to a boil, reduce the heat and simmer for 2 minutes.

4  Place two steaks on each warm serving plate. Remove the toothpicks or skewers, then top each steak with a spoonful of the tomato sauce.

**Serving suggestion**
Serve with garlic bruschetta, or steamed green beans and black olives.

## Variation

Sprinkle the tomato-topped steaks with grated mozzarella, then briefly melt the cheese under a hot grill (broiler).

# Take a steak and...

A simple steak is a great base to build a meal around. Keep a supply in the freezer, portioned for easy retrieval, and thaw them during the day. Served with a salad and boiled new potatoes, or dressed with a fancy sauce, a juicy steak is welcome any day.

## Sizzling steak secrets

Cooking steak is not difficult, but a few simple tips will ensure the best results.

● If you have time, take the meat from the fridge up to 30 minutes before cooking, so you are not putting chilled meat into a hot pan, which will reduce the pan temperature.

● To avoid smoke, oil the meat rather than the pan.

● Cook your steak in a heavy-based frying pan, or on a barbecue or chargrill.

● Preheat the pan so that the meat sears and starts to cook immediately. If your steak is thick, sear it over high heat, then reduce the heat slightly so it cooks through without burning.

● Don't keep turning the meat — once will do.

● Test for 'doneness' by pressing the meat with tongs — the firmer it is, the more well done it will be. (This can take a little practice.) The cooking time will depend on the thickness of the meat, and how well cooked you like it.

● To ensure tender, juicy meat, rest it after cooking. Transfer it to a plate, cover loosely with foil and let it stand for 5 minutes to allow the juices to reabsorb.

## Jazz it up!

### Drizzle with a juicy glaze

After you've cooked your steak, use the cooking juices left behind to make a flavoursome glaze. While the meat is resting, 'deglaze' the pan by adding about ½ cup (125 ml) beef stock and/or red or white wine to the pan. Swirl it around and scrape the bottom of the pan with a wooden spoon to dislodge and dissolve any yummy browned bits. Cook over medium heat for a couple of minutes to reduce slightly. Serve the glaze drizzled over the meat.

You can enhance the flavour of the glaze by adding some butter and crushed garlic and/or chopped fresh herbs, such as rosemary or thyme. Strain before serving, if desired.

## Make a luscious sauce or gravy

You can make a sauce using the same deglazing technique opposite. While the meat is resting, add ¼ cup (60 ml) beef stock and ½ cup (125 ml) pouring (light) cream to the frying pan — you can also add 1–2 tablespoons wholegrain mustard, and a little white wine or marsala if desired. Stir and simmer until thickened slightly.

For a gravy, add 1 tablespoon butter or oil to the pan. Sprinkle in 1 tablespoon plain (all-purpose) flour and cook over medium heat for 1 minute, stirring and scraping the base of the pan. Gradually add 1 cup (250 ml) beef stock, stirring well between each addition, until smooth. Simmer for 2 minutes, or until thickened.

## Add a dollop of flavoured butter

Make a flavoured butter and keep it in the freezer for use at any time. Beat 125 g (4 oz) butter until light and creamy, then stir in any of the following: 2 tablespoons mustard, 2 tablespoons chopped fresh herbs, 2 teaspoons finely grated lemon zest, 1 tablespoon grated horseradish, 2 crushed garlic cloves or 1 finely chopped red chilli. (You can also try different combinations of these flavourings.)

Serve straight away as a dollop, or for later use, shape the butter into a log on a sheet of foil or plastic wrap, then roll up and seal. Refrigerate or freeze the butter, then simply cut into discs to serve.

## Other flashy ideas

● Top a cooked steak with a piece of creamy blue cheese.

● Press cracked peppercorns onto the meat before cooking.

● Cut a pocket into the side of a thick steak, then fill it with pâté, flavoured butter, blue cheese or herbs.

● For a cheat's schnitzel, sprinkle thin cooked steaks with coarse breadcrumbs that have been pan-fried until crisp.

● Top a thin cooked steak with heated tomato pasta sauce and grated cheese. Grill briefly to melt the cheese.

● While the steaks rest, melt some butter in the pan, add fresh sage leaves and cook until the leaves are crisp and the butter is lightly browned. Serve with pork or veal.

● While the meat rests, sauté some halved cherry tomatoes with a crushed garlic clove. Add a dash of balsamic vinegar and serve over the steak.

# Lamb & chickpeas with chargrilled eggplant

**500 g (1 lb) minced (ground) lamb**

**3 teaspoons ground cumin**

**410 g (15 oz) can chopped tomatoes**

**420 g (15 oz) can chickpeas, drained**

**6 lady finger eggplants (aubergines)**

1   Heat 1 tablespoon olive oil in a large non-stick frying pan over high heat. Add the lamb and cook for about 2 minutes, breaking up the lumps with a wooden spoon. Letting any water cook away, stir the lamb for another 2 minutes, or until it browns. Transfer to a bowl.

2   Reduce the heat to medium. Heat another 1 tablespoon olive oil in the pan, add 2 teaspoons of the cumin and stir for 30 seconds. Add the tomatoes, browned lamb, chickpeas and ½ cup (125 ml) water and mix well. Reduce the heat to medium–low and simmer, uncovered, for 10 minutes, or until most of the liquid has evaporated.

3   Meanwhile, preheat a chargrill pan or grill (broiler) to medium–high. Halve each eggplant lengthwise, brush the cut surfaces with a little olive oil and sprinkle with the remaining cumin. Cook for 10 minutes, or until golden brown and tender. (If chargrilling, turn the slices halfway through.)

4   Serve the lamb mixture topped with the eggplant slices.

**Serving suggestion**
Serve a dollop of Greek-style yogurt, and soft flat bread, such as lavash.

## Variation
Replace the lamb with minced (ground) beef, and add a little chilli powder for added spice.

PREPARATION 10 minutes

COOKING 15 minutes

SERVES 4

## Shortcut ingredients
Canned legumes such as lentils, chickpeas and beans are a great time saver as they don't need soaking and precooking.

EACH SERVING PROVIDES
1165 kJ, 278 kcal, 31 g protein, 11 g fat (4 g saturated fat), 14 g carbohydrate (5 g sugars), 6 g fibre, 316 mg sodium

# Lamb, green bean & orange salad

Instead of lamb loin fillets, you can use shredded barbecued chicken, chargrilled sliced pork or chargrilled lamb cutlets in this salad. Add a handful of toasted walnut halves for extra crunch.

300 g (10 oz) whole baby green beans
8 lamb loin fillets
3 large oranges
½ cup (90 g) black olives
2–3 tablespoons ready-made French dressing

**PREPARATION** 10 minutes

**COOKING** 10 minutes

**SERVES** 4

## Shopping tip
If fresh beans are expensive, buy a small bag of frozen baby beans.

EACH SERVING PROVIDES
1123 kJ, 268 kcal, 19 g protein, 13 g fat
(4 g saturated fat), 18 g carbohydrate
(14 g sugars), 5 g fibre, 586 mg sodium

1  Top and tail the beans, then steam, microwave or boil them for 1–2 minutes, or until just softened. Drain and refresh under cold running water, then drain again. Cut the beans in half diagonally.

2  Meanwhile, brush the lamb fillets lightly with olive oil and season well with salt and freshly ground black pepper. Remove the rind and white pith from the oranges, then cut the oranges into slices 1 cm (½ inch) thick.

3  Heat a large frying pan over medium–high heat. Add the lamb and cook, without turning, for 2–3 minutes, or until small beads of moisture appear on top. Turn and cook the other side for 2–3 minutes. (You may need to turn the meat three times so that all the sides are browned and the lamb is cooked through.) Remove from the heat and leave to rest for 3 minutes.

4  Place the orange slices in a serving bowl or arrange on serving plates. Slice the lamb diagonally and gently toss it in a bowl with the beans, olives and dressing. Pile the salad over the orange slices and serve.

## Serving suggestion
Serve this lovely salad with plenty of crusty French bread.

## Variation
Instead of lamb loin fillets, you can use shredded barbecued chicken, chargrilled sliced pork, or chargrilled lamb loin chops or cutlets.

# Stir-fried lamb with ginger & broccolini

**PREPARATION** 10 minutes

**COOKING** 15 minutes

**SERVES** 4

## Variations

● Beef, pork or chicken will work well in this stir-fry too — choose a tender, lean cut and slice it into thin strips.

● Use oyster sauce or plum sauce instead of chilli sauce.

EACH SERVING PROVIDES
942 kJ, 225 kcal, 30 g protein, 8 g fat
(4 g saturated fat), 9 g carbohydrate
(4 g sugars), 2 g fibre, 239 mg sodium

500 g (1 lb) lamb leg steaks, lamb backstraps or loin fillets

2 cm (¾ inch) knob of fresh ginger

1 large onion

250 g (8 oz) broccolini

2 tablespoons mild chilli sauce

1 Cut the lamb across the grain into thin strips. Peel and finely chop the ginger. Cut the onion in half, then cut each half into six wedges. Trim the broccolini ends. Cut the broccolini stems from the tops, then cut the stems in half. Set aside.

2 Heat a wok or large frying pan over high heat. Add 1 tablespoon peanut or vegetable oil and swirl to coat. Working in two batches, stir-fry the lamb for 3 minutes, or until well browned and just cooked through, reheating the wok in between. Remove each batch to a plate.

3 Reheat the wok over medium–high heat. Add another 1 tablespoon oil, then stir-fry the onion for 1 minute, or until just beginning to soften. Add the ginger and stir-fry for 30 seconds. Add the broccolini stems, chilli sauce and ¼ cup (60 ml) water. Mix well, then cover and cook for 2 minutes.

4 Add the broccolini tops, the lamb and any juices, and another 1 tablespoon water if the mixture looks a little dry. Cover and cook for a further 3 minutes, or until the broccolini is tender–crisp, stirring halfway through. Serve immediately.

# Tandoori-style lamb cutlets

1 cup (250 g) Greek-style yogurt
⅓ cup (90 g) tandoori curry paste
12 frenched lamb cutlets
2 Lebanese or other small cucumbers
3 tablespoons chopped fresh mint

PREPARATION 10 minutes

COOKING 10 minutes

SERVES 4

1   Preheat a barbecue flatplate or chargrill plate to high, then brush with a little oil.

2   Meanwhile, whisk ¼ cup (60 g) of the yogurt with the tandoori paste, then brush over the cutlets. Peel and cut the cucumbers into small cubes. Combine in a small bowl with the mint and remaining yogurt.

3   Cook the cutlets for 3–4 minutes on each side, turning once only. Remove from the heat and leave to rest for 2 minutes. Serve hot, with the minted cucumber yogurt.

## Serving suggestion
Serve with steamed rice or Indian-style tandoor bread, and a side salad of mixed salad leaves tossed with slices of mango and red onion.

## Variation
Replace the lamb with boneless, skinless chicken breasts. Cut the chicken into 2 cm (¾ inch) cubes and thread onto skewers. Brush with the tandoori yogurt mixture and cook for 2–3 minutes on each of its four sides.

EACH SERVING PROVIDES
1377 kJ, 329 kcal, 31 g protein, 21 g fat (9 g saturated fat), 8 g carbohydrate (6 g sugars), 1 g fibre, 915 mg sodium

# Lamb cutlets with peperonata

12 frenched lamb cutlets
2 red capsicums (bell peppers)
1 green capsicum (bell pepper)
400 g (14 oz) ripe tomatoes
8 large basil leaves

1   Preheat a barbecue grill or chargrill pan to high. Meanwhile, lightly brush the lamb cutlets with a little olive oil and season with salt and freshly ground black pepper. Cut the capsicums lengthwise into thin strips. Chop the tomatoes, and roughly chop the basil. Set aside.

2   Heat a medium frying pan (one with a lid) over medium–high heat. Add 1 tablespoon olive oil, heat for 30 seconds, then add the capsicums and tomatoes. Cook, stirring, for 2 minutes, or until the tomatoes are just beginning to soften. Add ½ cup (125 ml) water, bring to a boil, then reduce the heat to medium. Cover and cook, stirring occasionally, for 2–3 minutes, or until the tomatoes are soft.

3   While the peperonata is cooking, chargrill the lamb cutlets, without turning, for 2–3 minutes, or until small beads of moisture appear on top. Turn and cook the other side until done to your liking. Remove the lamb from the heat and leave to rest for 3 minutes.

4   Stir the basil into the peperonata; taste and season with salt and freshly ground black pepper if needed. Serve with the lamb cutlets.

## Serving suggestion
Try some steamed English spinach, drizzled with good olive oil.

## Variations
•   Instead of lamb cutlets, you could also use pork cutlets, or boneless, skinless chicken breasts.
•   Replace the fresh tomatoes with a 500 g (1 lb) jar of tomato pasta sauce (preferably one containing onion or garlic).

PREPARATION 10 minutes
COOKING 10 minutes
SERVES 4

## Cook's tip
When pan-frying or using a wok, heat the pan or wok to the right temperature before you add the oil, then heat the oil before adding the first ingredient. This ensures the meat or vegetables cook quickly and evenly, and also colour and brown well.

EACH SERVING PROVIDES
956 kJ, 228 kcal, 28 g protein, 13 g fat (5 g saturated fat), 5 g carbohydrate (5 g sugars), 2 g fibre, 86 mg sodium

# Lamb leg steaks with orange sauce

PREPARATION 5 minutes

COOKING 15 minutes

SERVES 4

## Cook's tip

For meat to brown well and cook evenly, it should sizzle as it hits the pan or the barbecue.

EACH SERVING PROVIDES
1606 kJ, 384 kcal, 34 g protein, 17 g fat (9 g saturated fat), 24 g carbohydrate (24 g sugars), 2 g fibre, 173 mg sodium

4 lamb leg steaks or lamb rump steaks, about 150 g (5 oz) each
2 cloves garlic
2 large oranges
⅓ cup (100 g) orange marmalade
2 tablespoons butter

1 Trim the lamb steaks. Brush lightly with olive oil and season well with salt and freshly ground black pepper. Finely chop the garlic and set aside. Grate the zest from the oranges, then juice the oranges; place the juice and zest in a bowl and stir in the marmalade until combined.

2 Heat the butter in a large frying pan over medium–high heat until foaming. Add the lamb and cook, without turning, for 3–4 minutes, or until small beads of moisture appear on top. Turn and cook for a further 3 minutes for medium, or until done to your liking. Remove from the pan and leave to rest for 2–3 minutes.

3 Add the garlic to the pan and cook, stirring, for 1 minute. Stir in the marmalade mixture, then reduce the heat and simmer, uncovered, for 2–3 minutes, or until the sauce has reduced to a syrup-like glaze.

4 Return the steaks to the pan, coat them with the sauce and serve.

### Serving suggestion
This dish is lovely with steamed sugarsnap peas and some sautéed diced potatoes.

### Variations
- The sweet orange sauce is also great with chicken. Use uncrumbed chicken schnitzels, or pound boneless, skinless chicken breasts to a 1.5 cm (⅝ inch) thickness.
- Add a little grated fresh ginger with the garlic.

# Pork schnitzel with apple & mint salsa

Using a packaged stuffing mix for your crumb coating is a handy way to add extra flavour, as the stuffing mix will usually contain dried onion and herbs such as sage, thyme and marjoram.

**4 pork leg steaks, about 150 g (5 oz) each**

**2 eggs**

**2 cups (200 g) sage and onion stuffing mix**

**2 green apples**

**1 tablespoon chopped fresh mint**

1   Place each pork steak between two sheets of baking (parchment) paper or plastic wrap, then pound with a meat mallet or rolling pin to about a 5 mm (¼ inch) thickness. Whisk the eggs in a bowl with 2 tablespoons water and season with salt and freshly ground black pepper. Spread the stuffing mix on a large plate.

2   Dip the pork steaks in the beaten egg, then into the stuffing mixture, pressing the crumbs on gently. Lay them on a tray and refrigerate for 5 minutes. Meanwhile, peel, core and roughly chop the apples and place in a small bowl. Add the mint and toss through.

3   Pour enough vegetable oil into a large frying pan to come halfway up the side of the pan. Heat the oil over medium–high heat. When the oil is hot, cook two pork schnitzels for 3½ minutes on each side, turning them once only. Drain on paper towels and keep warm.

4   Reheat the oil and cook the remaining schnitzels. Serve with a spoonful of the apple and mint salsa.

## Serving suggestion
A radicchio and red onion salad would be great with the schnitzels.

## Variations
- Instead of pork, use chicken breast schnitzels.
- Replace the apple with pear or fresh mango.

**PREPARATION** 10 minutes

**COOKING** 15 minutes

**SERVES** 4

## Cook's tip
It is important to reheat the oil between batches, so the crumbed meat doesn't take up the oil and become soggy. To test if the oil is hot enough to cook in, place the tip of a wooden spoon handle in the oil. Bubbles should form all around the submerged handle.

EACH SERVING PROVIDES
1188 kJ, 284 kcal, 36 g protein, 9 g fat (3 g saturated fat), 14 g carbohydrate (10 g sugars), 2 g fibre, 252 mg sodium

# Barbecued pork skewers

**PREPARATION** 5 minutes

**COOKING** 10 minutes

**SERVES** 4

## Shopping tip

Ask your butcher what cut of pork he has used for his diced pork — for juicy skewers, a tender cut is preferable. Instead of ready-diced pork you could use pork leg, loin or fillet and cut it into 2.5 cm (1 inch) cubes.

EACH SERVING PROVIDES
1286 kJ, 308 kcal, 41 g protein, 14 g fat
(4 g saturated fat), 7 g carbohydrate
(2 g sugars), 2 g fibre, 469 mg sodium

Tapenade is made from black or green olives, capers, anchovies, garlic and herbs. You can use black or green tapenade here. You'll find it in jars at supermarkets, or you can easily make your own.

**750 g (1½ lb) lean diced pork**

**3 large limes**

**⅓ cup (90 g) black olive tapenade (see Basics)**

1  Preheat a barbecue flat plate or chargrill to medium–high. Meanwhile, cut the pork into 2.5 cm (1 inch) cubes. Take eight 20 cm (8 inch) metal skewers and thread five or six pieces of pork onto each. Take care not to pack the meat on too tightly — leave a little space around each piece so the heat can get to all sides as the meat cooks.

2  Grate the zest from one lime, then juice the lime. Place the zest and juice in a small bowl, add the tapenade and 1 tablespoon olive oil and stir to combine. Cut the remaining limes into wedges for serving.

3  Brush the hot barbecue plate or chargrill with a little oil. Brush the meat skewers evenly with the tapenade mixture, then place on the barbecue or chargrill and reduce the heat to medium. Cook for 8–10 minutes, or until cooked through, giving the skewers three turns so the pork is evenly cooked.

4  Remove the skewers from the heat and leave to rest for 2 minutes. Serve with the lime wedges.

### Serving suggestion
Coleslaw goes well with these skewers — you could simply use a supermarket packet of shredded red cabbage and carrot and toss it with a little Italian dressing just before serving.

### Variation
Replace the pork with cubes of a firm-fleshed fish such as tuna or swordfish. The fish will need less cooking time — don't overcook it or it will fall apart.

# Pork with creamy garlic mustard sauce

**PREPARATION** 5 minutes

**COOKING** 15 minutes

**SERVES** 4

## Variations

● Serve the sauce with pan-fried chicken breast schnitzels.
● Add lemon zest or herbs such as chives or parsley to the sauce.
● For a thicker sauce, add a teaspoon of cornflour (cornstarch) to the cold cream.

EACH SERVING PROVIDES
1555 kJ, 371 kcal, 44 g protein, 19 g fat
(10 g saturated fat), 5 g carbohydrate
(3 g sugars), <1 g fibre, 311 mg sodium

**4 pork butterfly steaks, about 200 g (7 oz) each**

**2–3 large cloves garlic**

**¼ cup (60 g) wholegrain mustard**

**½ cup (125 ml) chicken stock**

**¾ cup (180 ml) cream**

1 Trim the pork steaks, brush lightly with olive oil and season well with salt and freshly ground black pepper. Thinly slice the garlic.

2 Heat a large non-stick frying pan over medium–high heat. Add the pork and cook, without turning, for 3–4 minutes, or until small beads of moisture appear on top. Turn and cook for a further 3–4 minutes for medium, or until done to your liking. Remove from the pan and leave to rest for 2–3 minutes.

3 Heat a little olive oil in the pan. Add the garlic and cook, stirring constantly, until the garlic just begins to colour. Add the mustard, stock and cream. Reduce the heat and simmer, uncovered, for 3–4 minutes, or until the sauce has reduced and thickened, stirring often.

4 Place the pork on serving plates, spoon the sauce over and serve.

# Pork cassoulet

8–10 thin pork sausages
8 spring onions (scallions)
420 g (15 oz) can cannellini beans
750 g (1½ lb) jar of tomato passata (puréed tomatoes)
5 fresh thyme sprigs, or 1 teaspoon dried thyme or marjoram

1  Heat a frying pan over medium heat. Add a little olive oil, then add the sausages and fry for 2–3 minutes, or until golden, turning often. Remove the sausages and cut each one in three.

2  Trim the spring onions and cut them into 5 cm (2 inch) lengths. Drain and rinse the beans. Place the spring onions and beans in a heavy-based saucepan or flameproof casserole dish with the passata, thyme and ½ cup (125 ml) water.

3  Bring to a boil over medium–high heat, then reduce the heat to medium–low. Add the sausages, partially cover the pan and cook, stirring occasionally, for 10 minutes, or until the sausages are cooked through and the sauce has thickened slightly. Serve hot.

## Serving suggestion
Serve with a crusty baguette and green salad.

PREPARATION 10 minutes

COOKING 15 minutes

SERVES 4

## Variations
- Use 4 pork chops instead of sausages, or a mix of both.
- Add a sliced chorizo sausage for a little spice.

EACH SERVING PROVIDES
1859 kJ, 444 kcal, 22 g protein, 29 g fat (12 g saturated fat), 22 g carbohydrate (12 g sugars), 10 g fibre, 1729 mg sodium

meat

167

# Pork & mango curry

**PREPARATION** 5 minutes

**COOKING** 15 minutes

**SERVES** 4

## Shopping tip
Check that the stir-fry pork strips are from a tender cut of pork. Instead of ready-cut pork strips, you could use pork leg, loin or fillet; cut the pork thinly across the grain into thin strips.

EACH SERVING PROVIDES
2111 kJ, 505 kcal, 35 g protein, 36 g fat
(16 g saturated fat), 10 g carbohydrate
(9 g sugars), 1 g fibre, 124 mg sodium

Using a prepared curry paste makes cooking curries almost a one-step process. Canned mango pulp gives all the sweetness and texture of mango when fresh mangoes are not in season.

**750 g (1½ lb) lean pork stir-fry strips**

**2 tablespoons mild curry paste, such as korma or rendang**

**425 g (15 oz) can mango slices, drained**

**140 ml (4½ fl oz) can coconut cream**

**fresh coriander (cilantro) sprigs, to serve**

1　Place the pork in a bowl, add 1½ tablespoons vegetable oil and mix well. Heat a large heavy-based frying pan over high heat. Working in three batches, fry the pork for 2–3 minutes, or until just cooked. Remove each batch to a plate.

2　Add another 1 tablespoon oil to the pan. Reduce the heat to low, add the curry paste and cook, stirring, for 2 minutes. Stir in the mango pulp, then the coconut cream. Increase the heat to medium and simmer, stirring often, for 2 minutes.

3　Return the pork to the pan and simmer for 2 minutes to heat through — do not allow to boil. Taste and season with salt and freshly ground black pepper if needed. Serve sprinkled with coriander.

### Serving suggestion
Offer steamed jasmine rice (Thai fragrant rice), and stir-fried Asian greens such as baby bok choy.

### Variation
Add toasted flaked coconut as an additional garnish.

# Pork & mushroom stir-fry

750 g (1½ lb) piece of pork fillet
200 g (7 oz) oyster mushrooms
250 g (8 oz) snow peas (mangetout)
¼ cup (60 ml) sweet sherry, white wine or chicken stock
½ cup (125 ml) black bean sauce

1   Cut the pork across the grain into thin strips. Place in a bowl and season with salt and freshly ground black pepper. Trim the base of the mushrooms. Top and tail the snow peas, then cut them in half.

2   Heat a wok or large frying pan over high heat. Add 1 tablespoon peanut or vegetable oil and swirl to coat. Working in two batches, fry the pork for 3 minutes, or until well browned and just cooked through. Remove each batch to a plate.

3   Reheat the wok and add another 1 tablespoon oil. Add the mushrooms and snow peas and stir-fry for 1–2 minutes. Pour in the sherry and cook until it has reduced a little, then add the black bean sauce and stir until it simmers.

4   Return the pork to the wok and toss to warm through. Serve hot.

### Serving suggestion
Serve with steamed rice or stir-fried egg or rice noodles.

## Variation
Try this recipe with beef.

PREPARATION 10 minutes

COOKING 10 minutes

SERVES 4

## Shopping tip
Ask your butcher to cut the pork into stir-fry strips for you. You could use pork leg, loin or pork scotch steaks instead of fillet.

EACH SERVING PROVIDES
1269 kJ, 303 kcal, 45 g protein, 5 g fat
(2 g saturated fat), 13 g carbohydrate
(10 g sugars), 5 g fibre, 1447 mg sodium

# Pork with cabbage & apple sauté

2 green apples, such as granny smith
500 g (1 lb) savoy cabbage (about ¼ of a whole cabbage)
1 large red onion
1 teaspoon sweet paprika
4 thick pork loin cutlets, about 200 g (7 oz) each

PREPARATION 10 minutes

COOKING 10 minutes

SERVES 4

## Cook's tip

For this recipe you could also use pork loin or pork scotch fillets instead of cutlets.

EACH SERVING PROVIDES
1268 kJ, 303 kcal, 45 g protein, 4 g fat
(2 g saturated fat), 19 g carbohydrate
(13 g sugars), 6 g fibre, 113 mg sodium

1  Peel, halve and core the apples, then cut into thin wedges. Coarsely shred the cabbage. Halve and thinly slice the onion.

2  Heat 1 tablespoon olive oil in a saucepan over medium heat. Add the onion and cook, stirring, for 2 minutes. Stir in the apple, cabbage, paprika and ½ cup (125 ml) water. Increase the heat to medium–high, bring to a boil, then cover and cook for 5 minutes, or until the cabbage is just tender, stirring once or twice. Season well with salt and freshly ground black pepper.

3  Meanwhile, preheat a chargrill pan to high. Brush the pork cutlets lightly with olive oil and season well with salt and pepper. Add the cutlets and cook, without turning, for 3–4 minutes, or until small beads of moisture appear on top. Turn and cook until done to your liking, then remove from the heat and leave to rest for 3–4 minutes.

4  Serve the pork with the cabbage and apple sauté.

## Serving suggestion
Crispy fried potatoes would be just the thing!

## Variations
- Replace the savoy with red cabbage, or apples with pears.
- Add some chopped prunes or grated orange zest to the sauté.
- Replace the water with apple juice or apple cider; use caraway seeds instead of paprika.

seafood

# Succulent seafood parcels

Cooking a whole fish or fillets of fish in parcels ensures that all the lovely cooking juices are retained, keeping the seafood moist. It is also an elegant way to present the fish — and unwrapping the parcels at the dinner table is always a delight.

Cooking fish in parcels couldn't be simpler. See our tips below, and have fun experimenting by adding different flavourings to the parcel to infuse the fish.

- Nearly any seafood can be 'wrapped' (see the wrapper ideas in the box below) and then baked, barbecued or steamed. Most cooking methods will require 10–15 minutes.

- Ensure the parcel is securely closed, so none of the precious cooking juices can leak out.

- If placing the parcel over direct heat, such as a barbecue plate, turn the parcel halfway through cooking. If the parcel is steamed or baked on a rack in an oven or hooded barbecue, you won't need to turn it.

- For each person, allow a 150–180 g (5–6 oz) fish fillet or steak, a 180–200 g (6–7 oz) cutlet, or a small (350–500 g/12 oz–1 lb) plate-sized whole fish.

### Edible wrappers

- Wrap the fish in edible leaves, such as vine, cabbage or lettuce leaves.

- Encase the fish in thawed frozen pastry, such as puff, shortcrust or filo pastry.

### Inedible wrappers

- Wrap the fish in baking (parchment) paper, then foil (you won't need any oil). Wrapping the fish in baking paper first ensures any citrus juices won't react with the foil and impart a metallic taste.

 If you have access to them, you can also use banana leaves. First blanch the banana leaves in boiling water for 30 seconds to soften them.

**Lemon & herbs**   Scatter sliced lemon or lime over the fish, and some fresh or dried herbs such as parsley, dill, chives or oregano. Optional extras include chopped spring onions (scallions), garlic, butter and a splash of wine or verjuice.

**Fish in pastry**   Spread dijon mustard over a fish fillet and sprinkle with fresh dill. Wrap in puff pastry or 4 lightly oiled filo pastry sheets. Bake in a preheated 200°C (400°F/Gas 6) oven for 15 minutes, or until the pastry is golden. Serve with steamed beans or asparagus.

**Moroccan fish with couscous**   Dust the fish with Moroccan spice mix (see Basics), or a similar spice mix, and drizzle with lime juice. Place on a bed of prepared couscous, tossed with sultanas (golden raisins) and coriander (cilantro) leaves, before wrapping.

**Yummy curry fish**   Coat the fish in your favourite curry paste, drizzle with coconut milk or cream and top with mint leaves before wrapping. Serve with steamed rice.

**Thai-style fish with rice noodles**   Lay the fish on prepared noodles; drizzle with lime juice and sweet chilli sauce or coconut milk. Sprinkle with shredded Kaffir lime leaves or coriander (cilantro) before wrapping.

**Fish with mixed mushrooms**   Top the fish with lemon slices, fresh thyme and sliced mixed mushrooms, such as enoki, shiitake and Swiss brown. Place on finely sliced leeks before wrapping.

# Fresh from the sea

When you're short of time, seafood makes a perfect meal as it requires so little preparation, is quick and easy to cook by a variety of methods, and can simply be served with lemon or lime wedges and a sprinkling of fresh or dried herbs.

To get the very best out of seafood, follow a few simple rules: buy the freshest possible, store it correctly, use it (or freeze it) as quickly as possible — and never overcook it!

## How to tell if seafood is fresh

All seafood should have a fresh sea smell, but not smell 'fishy', and have a firm texture and good lustre or shine. Whole fish should have a firm, bright eye (not sunken) and bright red gills. Fillets should have no brown markings and shouldn't be dried out around the edges. It's a good idea to shop where there is a high turnover, because the seafood is replenished more often and will therefore be fresher.

## How to store seafood

Seafood should be kept cold and refrigerated as quickly as possible after purchase. Take a chiller bag with an ice pack to transport your purchased seafood, or ask the shop to wrap some ice with your seafood. To reduce chilling time, remove any paper wrapping from seafood parcels before refrigerating. Mussels should be stored in the warmest part of the refrigerator.

Consume fish within 2–3 days and prawns (shrimp) and mussels within 1–2 days, but remember that all fresh seafood is best used as soon as possible.

## Cooking

Seafood can be barbecued, baked, grilled (broiled), steamed, poached and even smoked, but the cooking time is often shorter than you think. Remember to allow for retained heat once the seafood is removed from the heat, as it will continue cooking.

Thicker pieces should be cooked at a lower temperature, so the outside doesn't burn or dry out before the middle has a chance to cook through.

## Substituting seafood

Don't be afraid to experiment with different seafood in recipes. If unsure, ask your local fishmonger about substitutes and quantities. They have the seafood knowledge and are more than happy to share it.

# Chorizo scallops

This simple but flavoursome dish is ideal for casual entertaining. Try tossing the cooked chorizo and scallops through hot linguine.

1 tablespoon cumin seeds
1 chorizo sausage, about 125 g (4 oz)
500 g (1 lb) scallops, cleaned and deveined
1 lemon
½ cup (30 g) chopped fresh parsley

1  Put the cumin seeds in a small pan and heat for 2–3 minutes, or until they become fragrant. Grind into a fine powder using a mortar and pestle or a spice grinder. Set aside.

2  Thinly slice the chorizo. If the scallops are large, cut them in half, otherwise leave them whole. Juice the lemon and set aside.

3  Heat a frying pan over medium heat. Add the chorizo and fry without any oil (the chorizo will release its own oil) for 2 minutes, or until crisp on both sides. Remove to a bowl.

4  In the same pan, fry the scallops in the chorizo oil for 1 minute on each side. (You may need to cook them in batches; don't crowd the pan or they will 'stew'.) Return the chorizo to the pan with any juices. Stir in the lemon juice, cumin and parsley, heat through briefly and serve.

**Serving suggestion**
Delicious with thinly sliced fresh or cooked fennel, or a side salad.

## Variations
- Substitute the scallops with prawns.
- Add some chopped garlic or chilli to the mixture.

PREPARATION 10 minutes

COOKING 10 minutes

SERVES 4

## Cook's tip
For a softer texture, the skin of the chorizo sausage can be peeled off before cooking.

EACH SERVING PROVIDES
699 kJ, 167 kcal, 19 g protein, 7 g fat
(3 g saturated fat), 5 g carbohydrate
(1 g sugars), 1 g fibre, 569 mg sodium

seafood

# Roasted salmon with greens

PREPARATION 10 minutes

COOKING 15 minutes

SERVES 4

## Cook's tip

Piri piri is a Portuguese-style spice mix based on chilli — use with care as it can be quite hot!

## Quick tip

For an effortless and delicious meal, make sure you preheat the oven and boil a kettle of water before preparation.

EACH SERVING PROVIDES
1340 kJ, 320 kcal, 34 g protein, 11 g fat (2 g saturated fat), 20 g carbohydrate (2 g sugars), 4 g fibre, 73 mg sodium

8 small new potatoes, about 500 g (1 lb) in total
1 tablespoon piri piri spice mix
4 x 150 g (5 oz) salmon fillets, skin removed
150 g (5 oz) green beans
150 g (5 oz) sugarsnap peas

1  Preheat the oven to 220°C (425°F/Gas 7). Line two baking trays with baking (parchment) paper.

2  Cut the potatoes lengthwise into wedges and place in a large bowl. Toss with 1 tablespoon olive oil and some salt and freshly ground black pepper and place on one of the baking trays in a single layer. Rub the spice mix evenly over each side of the salmon portions. Place them on the other baking tray, then drizzle each portion with ½ teaspoon olive oil. Roast the potatoes for 15 minutes, and the salmon for 8–10 minutes, depending on their thickness.

3  While the fish is roasting, half-fill an electric kettle with water and bring to a boil. String the beans and cut them in half if they are long; string the peas. Pour some boiling water into a saucepan and bring back to a boil over medium–high heat. Add the beans and peas and cook for 2–3 minutes, or until just tender. Drain, then toss with a little olive oil, salt and freshly ground black pepper.

4  Serve the salmon with the potatoes, beans and peas.

## Variations

- Use another spice mix, such as Moroccan, lemon pepper or Cajun (see Basics).
- Instead of salmon you could use thick portions of firm white fish fillets, such as barramundi, blue-eye trevalla, haddock or pollock.

# Salt & pepper calamari

We've 'honeycombed' the calamari by cutting a diamond pattern in the skin, but if you prefer you can cut the calamari tubes into thin rings, or just buy calamari rings. You can also cook the calamari on a chargrill pan or barbecue.

**2 Lebanese or other small cucumbers**

**2 tablespoons rice vinegar**

**2 teaspoons caster (superfine) sugar**

**750 g (1½ lb) calamari tubes**

**2 tablespoons lemon pepper (see Basics)**

1   Thinly slice the cucumbers and place on paper towels to drain. In a bowl, combine the rice vinegar, sugar and ¼ teaspoon salt and mix until the sugar has dissolved. Toss the cucumber with the vinegar.

2   Cut along one side of the calamari hoods and open flat. Wipe firmly with a paper towel. Using a sharp knife, lightly score the skin with a series of parallel lines on the diagonal, being careful not to cut all the way through. Cut another series of shallow lines at right angles to the first diagonal lines, to make a diamond shape (this makes the calamari curl as it cooks.) Now cut the calamari into pieces about 5 cm (2 inches) long and toss them in a bowl with half the lemon pepper until coated.

3   Heat a large frying pan over high heat, then oil the pan well. Once the oil is hot, add the calamari in batches and cook for 1–2 minutes, turning once — the calamari is cooked as soon as it turns white.

4   Sprinkle the calamari with the remaining lemon pepper and serve with the cucumber salad.

## Variations

●  Dip the calamari pieces in lightly beaten eggwhite, then tapioca starch, and deep-fry over high heat for 2–3 minutes, or until golden. Sprinkle with salt and freshly ground black pepper and serve.
●  Add some avocado, mango and/or watercress sprigs to the salad and serve with steamed jasmine rice (Thai fragrant rice).

PREPARATION 10 minutes

COOKING 10 minutes

SERVES 4

## Cook's tips

●  To intensify the flavour of the salt and pepper mix, heat it in a dry frying pan over medium heat before using.
●  For even more tender calamari, cover them with plastic wrap and gently hit them with a meat mallet before cooking.

EACH SERVING PROVIDES
860 kJ, 205 kcal, 32 g protein, 7 g fat (1 g saturated fat), 6 g carbohydrate (4 g sugars), 1 g fibre, 1907 mg sodium

seafood

# Smoked fish pâté

PREPARATION 10 minutes

COOKING none

SERVES 4

## Variation

Try adding some horseradish cream, baby capers, cornichons or gherkins (pickles), grated nutmeg and/or cayenne pepper to the fish mixture.

EACH SERVING PROVIDES
1961 kJ, 468 kcal, 22 g protein, 41 g fat (15 g saturated fat), 2 g carbohydrate (2 g sugars), <1 g fibre, 803 mg sodium

1 whole smoked mackerel or trout, about 400 g (14 oz)

½ cup (125 g) sour cream

⅓ cup (80 g) ricotta

1 lemon

3 tablespoons chopped fresh dill

1   Peel the skin off the fish and pull the flesh away from the bones. Discard the skin and bones and place the flesh in a large bowl. Add the sour cream and ricotta.

2   Zest and juice the lemon. Add 1 teaspoon lemon zest, 1 tablespoon lemon juice and the dill to the fish. Season with salt and freshly ground black pepper and mix together, keeping some of the chunkiness. Taste and add extra lemon juice, salt or pepper if desired.

3   Spoon the mixture into one large dish, or into individual bowls or ramekins. Cover and refrigerate until required. This pâté will keep for up to 3 days.

### Serving suggestion
Serve on thin toast or crackers, garnished with small watercress sprigs.

seafood

# Sashimi tuna with avocado in lettuce cups

400 g (14 oz) skinless sashimi-grade tuna

1 large avocado

¾ cup (185 g) wasabi mayonnaise (see Basics)

8 baby cos (romaine) lettuce leaves

2 tablespoons salmon roe

PREPARATION 10 minutes

COOKING none

SERVES 4 as a starter, or
2 as a main

## Shopping tip

Raw fish suitable for sashimi is sold in selected fishmongers and labelled 'sashimi grade', which means it can be eaten raw.

EACH SERVING PROVIDES
1171 kJ, 280 kcal, 13 g protein, 25 g fat (5 g saturated fat), <1 g carbohydrate (<1 g sugars), <1 g fibre, 139 mg sodium

1 Dice the tuna and avocado and place in a large bowl. Add the mayonnaise and very gently fold through the mixture until combined.

2 Spoon the mixture into the lettuce cups. Garnish with the salmon roe and serve immediately.

## Serving suggestion

Top with roasted black sesame seeds, or red or pink pickled ginger.

seafood

185

# Seafood ravioli

**300 g (10 oz) peeled and deveined uncooked prawns (shrimp)**
**4 canned water chestnuts**
**3 spring onions (scallions)**
**1 cup (250 ml) sesame ginger soy sauce**
**20 won ton or gow gee (egg dumpling) wrappers**

1 Bring a large pot of water to a simmer and cover until needed.

2 Meanwhile, chop the prawns and water chestnuts, and thinly slice the spring onions. Set one-third of the sliced spring onions aside as a garnish. Put half the prawns and water chestnuts and half the remaining spring onion in a food processor, then pulse until the mixture is finely chopped and sticking together. Transfer to a bowl and stir in the remaining prawns, water chestnuts, spring onions and 2 tablespoons of the soy sauce.

3 Place half the wrappers on a clean work surface, keeping the remaining wrappers covered with a damp cloth until required. Put 1 tablespoon of the filling on one side of the wrapper. Lightly brush the edges of the wrapper with water, then fold the wrapper over the filling. Gently force as much air out as possible and press the edges to seal. Repeat with the remaining filling and wrappers.

4 Place the parcels in the simmering water — make sure the water isn't boiling or the wrappers may fall apart. Cook for 4–5 minutes, or until they float to the surface.

5 Drain the ravioli and serve immediately, drizzled with the remaining soy sauce and garnished with the remaining spring onions.

## Variations

- Instead of (or as well as) prawns, use minced (ground) chicken or pork.
- Substitute bamboo shoots for the water chestnuts, and coriander (cilantro) for the spring onions.
- Instead of sesame ginger soy sauce, use a mixture of sweet chilli or soy sauce, sesame oil and grated fresh ginger.
- The filled wrappers can also be steamed for 6–8 minutes, or until cooked through; they can also be served in soup.

PREPARATION 10 minutes

COOKING 5 minutes

SERVES 4 (makes 20)

## Cook's tip

If you are preparing the ravioli in advance, dip the bottom of the filled wrappers in a little cornflour (cornstarch) to stop them becoming soggy. The prepared or cooked wrappers can be refrigerated for up to 2 days, or frozen for up to 1 month.

EACH SERVING PROVIDES
1204 kJ, 288 kcal, 25 g protein, 1 g fat (<1 g saturated fat), 40 g carbohydrate (2 g sugars), 2 g fibre, 4587 mg sodium

# Thai fish cakes

PREPARATION 10 minutes

COOKING 10 minutes

SERVES 4 (makes 20)

## Cook's tip

Redfish is traditionally used for fish cakes because the chopped flesh holds together well. If using other fish, add 1 small egg to the mixture for a firmer texture.

EACH SERVING PROVIDES
568 kJ, 140 kcal, 27 g protein, 3 g fat (1 g saturated fat), 1 g carbohydrate (<1 g sugars), <1 g fibre, 122 mg sodium

75 g (2½ oz) snake beans or green beans (5–6 snake beans, or 10–12 green beans)
2 makrut (kaffir lime) leaves
500 g (1 lb) boned, skinless fish fillets, such as redfish, ling, flathead, blue-eye trevalla, kingfish, haddock or pollock
2 tablespoons red curry paste
lime wedges, to serve

1   Top and tail the beans, then finely slice them. Remove the thick spine from the lime leaves, then finely slice the leaves. Cut the fish into chunks. Place the fish and curry paste in a food processor and pulse until coarsely chopped, but holding together. Scoop the mixture into a bowl and mix the beans and lime leaves through.

2   Heat a large frying pan over medium heat. Wet your hands, shaking off any excess water, and shape the mixture into 12 thin patties.

3   Add enough vegetable oil to coat the frying pan. Once the oil is hot, cook the patties, in batches if necessary, for 3–4 minutes on each side, or until the flesh changes colour from translucent to opaque.

4   Serve the fish cakes hot, with lime wedges for squeezing over.

## Variations

- Use Thai basil or coriander (cilantro) instead of lime leaves.
- Deep-fry the fish cakes for 3–4 minutes, until they turn golden and the flesh turns opaque.

# Ginger baked fish

PREPARATION 10 minutes

COOKING 15 minutes

SERVES 4

## Shopping tip

Pick the freshest fish you can find. Good varieties for baking whole include snapper, bream, flounder, halibut, mackerel, haddock and pollock.

## Quick tip

Use fish fillets instead of whole fish and reduce the cooking time to about 10 minutes.

EACH SERVING PROVIDES
1598 kJ, 382 kcal, 73 g protein, 8 g fat
(2 g saturated fat), 5 g carbohydrate
(2 g sugars), 1 g fibre, 858 mg sodium

4 cm (1½ inch) knob of fresh ginger
4 spring onions (scallions)
4 small, gutted, plate-sized fish, about 350 g (12 oz) each
¼ cup (60 ml) Japanese soy sauce, plus extra for drizzling
2 limes

1  Preheat the oven to 220°C (425°F/Gas 7).

2  Peel and julienne the ginger, and thinly slice the spring onions. On each fish, make two or three diagonal slices through the thickest part of the flesh. Brush each fish all over with oil (sesame oil is especially good if you have it), then place each fish on a sheet of baking (parchment) paper, on top of a sheet of foil. Scatter the ginger, spring onions and some salt and freshly ground black pepper over each fish and in the stomach cavities. Drizzle with the soy sauce.

3  Enclose the baking paper around each fish, twisting the ends securely, then wrap the foil around each fish. Place the fish parcels on a large baking tray and bake for 15 minutes, or until the flesh flakes easily when tested with a fork.

4  Cut the limes into wedges and serve with the fish, with some extra soy sauce for drizzling.

## Variations

● Scatter sliced limes or lemons inside and over the fish, or drizzle with lemon juice inside and out.
● Add sliced chillies, coriander (cilantro), lemongrass and/or garlic.
● The whole fish can also be steamed, although this may take a little longer — usually about 15–20 minutes, depending on the size.

seafood

# Salmon steaks with watercress salad

**250 g (8 oz) cherry or grape tomatoes**

**1 avocado**

**3 cups (90 g) watercress sprigs**

**¼ cup (60 ml) sushi vinegar**

**4 thin, skinless salmon steaks (or firm white fish fillets such as blue-eye trevalla, snapper, ling, barramundi, kingfish or pollock)**

1   Cut the tomatoes in half and place in a large salad bowl. Peel and dice the avocado. Add to the tomatoes with the watercress sprigs and vinegar and gently toss.

2   Meanwhile, preheat a barbecue or frying pan over medium–high heat. Lightly oil the salmon steaks and season with salt and freshly ground black pepper. Cook for 2–4 minutes on each side, depending on their thickness and how well done you like your salmon.

3   Divide the salad among shallow serving bowls. Arrange the salmon steaks over the top of each salad and serve.

## Variations

- Add diced mango or cucumber to the salad.
- Toss some blanched sugarsnap peas through the salad.

PREPARATION 10 minutes

COOKING 10 minutes

SERVES 4

## Cook's tip

To make your own sushi vinegar, combine 2 tablespoons rice vinegar, 1 tablespoon caster (superfine) sugar and ½ teaspoon salt in a small saucepan. Stir over low heat until the sugar has dissolved.

EACH SERVING PROVIDES
1780 kJ, 425 kcal, 41 g protein, 28 g fat (6 g saturated fat), 2 g carbohydrate (2 g sugars), 3 g fibre, 107 mg sodium

seafood

# Sardines with white bean mash

PREPARATION 10 minutes

COOKING 10 minutes

SERVES 4

## Cook's tip

To butterfly whole sardines, first cut the heads off. Cut along the stomach, then clean out the intestines with paper towels. Place the fish on a board cut side down, then push gently to flatten. Turn the fish over and pull out the backbone, snapping it as close to the tail as possible. Rinse the fish and pat dry with paper towels.

EACH SERVING PROVIDES
1508 kJ, 360 kcal, 35 g protein, 10 g fat
(2 g saturated fat), 25 g carbohydrate
(9 g sugars), 16 g fibre, 527 mg sodium

You can buy sardines already butterflied at some fishmongers, but if you can't find them you can easily butterfly them at home.

**400 g (14 oz) thin asparagus spears**

**250 g (8 oz) cherry tomatoes**

**2 tablespoons balsamic vinegar**

**3 x 420 g (15 oz) cans white beans, such as cannellini**

**12 butterflied fresh sardines**

1  Preheat the oven to 220°C (425°F/Gas 7). Line a large, shallow baking dish with baking (parchment) paper. Trim the asparagus, and cut the tomatoes in half across the middle. Place the asparagus and tomatoes in the baking dish and drizzle with the vinegar and 2 tablespoons extra virgin olive oil. Sprinkle with salt and freshly ground black pepper, toss gently to coat, then bake for 10 minutes.

2  Meanwhile, drain the beans, then rinse and drain again. Pour ¼ cup (60 ml) extra virgin olive oil into a saucepan and place over medium–low heat. Add the beans and allow to warm through, stirring and squashing the beans with a fork or a hand-held stick blender. Taste and season with salt and pepper, if required.

3  Heat a frying pan over medium–high heat. Pat the sardines dry with paper towels and season with salt and freshly ground black pepper. Lightly oil the frying pan. Once the oil is hot, add the sardines, in batches if necessary, and cook for 1 minute. Turn them over and fry for a further 1 minute, or until just cooked. (Alternatively, bake the sardines on a baking tray lined with baking paper for the final 3–4 minutes with the tomatoes and asparagus.)

4  Spoon the bean mash onto serving plates. Top with the asparagus, sardines and tomatoes. Drizzle with any baking or pan juices and serve.

## Variations
- Add chopped garlic, rosemary, lemon zest or lemon juice to the mash.
- Grate some parmesan over the vegetables.

# Parmesan-crusted fish

## Cook's tip

It's important not to use thick fish fillets for this recipe, as the parmesan is likely to burn before the fish cooks through.

EACH SERVING PROVIDES
1031 kJ, 246 kcal, 39 g protein, 7 g fat (3 g saturated fat), 6 g carbohydrate (<1 g sugars), <1 g fibre, 283 mg sodium

**4 thin fish fillets, such as bream, snapper, whiting, flathead, garfish, halibut or flounder, about 150 g (5 oz) each**

**⅓ cup (35 g) grated parmesan**

**¼ cup (35 g) plain (all-purpose) flour**

**1 egg**

**tzatziki or tartare sauce (see Basics), to serve**

1  Heat a frying pan over medium–high heat. Pour enough olive oil into the frying pan to coat the base, then heat for 1 minute.

2  Meanwhile, pat the fish dry with paper towels. Put the parmesan, flour and some salt and freshly ground black pepper in a clean plastic bag and shake to combine. Lightly beat the egg in a bowl. Dip the fish fillets in the egg, allowing the excess to drain off, then add them to the flour mixture, shaking gently to coat.

3  Add the fish to the pan and cook for 2 minutes on each side, or until golden. Serve immediately, with the tzatziki.

**Serving suggestion**
Serve with a salad and lemon wedges.

## Variations

- Add dried herbs to the flour.
- The fish could also be coated with fresh or dry breadcrumbs.

# Moroccan-style fish with herb couscous

PREPARATION 10 minutes

COOKING 10 minutes

SERVES 4

## Cook's tip

Instead of flavouring the couscous with the lemon zest and juice, you could throw in some chopped green olives and preserved lemon rind.

EACH SERVING PROVIDES
2188 kJ, 522 kcal, 44 g protein, 5 g fat (1 g saturated fat), 74 g carbohydrate (<1 g sugars), 1 g fibre, 111 mg sodium

4 firm white fish fillets, such as blue-eye trevalla, snapper, ling, barramundi, kingfish, haddock or pollock

2 tablespoons Moroccan spice mix (see Basics)

2 cups (370 g) couscous

1 lemon

4 tablespoons chopped coriander (cilantro), plus extra for sprinkling

1 Half-fill an electric kettle with water and bring to a boil. Pat the fish dry with paper towels, then sprinkle the spice mix all over the fish. Place the couscous in a large bowl, add 2 cups (500 ml) of the boiling water and set aside. Zest and juice the lemon.

2 Heat a large frying pan over medium heat. Lightly oil the pan, and once the oil is hot, add the fish and cook for 3–4 minutes on each side, or until the flesh flakes easily when tested with a fork.

3 Fluff the couscous with a fork, breaking up any lumps. Add the coriander, 1 teaspoon lemon zest, all the lemon juice, some salt and freshly ground black pepper and a good drizzle of olive oil. Mix well.

4 Serve the fish on a bed of couscous, sprinkled with extra coriander.

# Fast fish patties

1 lemon
420 g (15 oz) can cannellini beans
1 small egg
425 g (15 oz) can salmon or tuna
mayonnaise, sweet chilli sauce, aïoli or tzatziki (see Basics),
  to serve

1  Zest the lemon. Drain and rinse the beans, then place in a food processor. Add the egg, lemon zest, some salt and cracked black pepper and blend to a purée. Transfer the mixture to a bowl. Drain the salmon well, add to the bean mixture and mix well with a fork.

2  Wet your hands, shaking off any excess water, then shape the mixture into eight small, flat patties. (These patties can be made a day or several hours ahead; cover and refrigerate until required.)

3  Heat a large frying pan over medium heat. Add enough vegetable oil to coat the pan. Once the oil is hot, cook the patties, in two batches if necessary, for 3–4 minutes on each side, or until cooked through — be careful turning them as they are very soft. Drain on paper towels.

4  Serve the patties hot, with your choice of condiment.

PREPARATION 10 minutes

COOKING 10 minutes

SERVES 4 (makes 8 patties)

## Variations

●  Replace the cannellini beans with mashed potato or orange sweet potato, breadcrumbs or crushed matzo meal.
●  Add chopped spring onions (scallions), fresh herbs or chilli to the fish mixture.

EACH SERVING PROVIDES
970 kJ, 232 kcal, 24 g protein, 12 g fat
(3 g saturated fat), 7 g carbohydrate
(1 g sugars), 5 g fibre, 280 mg sodium

seafood

# Pan-fried fish with tomatoes & asparagus

**8 asparagus spears**

**250 g (8 oz) yellow or red grape or cherry tomatoes**

**1 tablespoon small salted capers**

**2 lemons**

**4 x 150 g (5 oz) firm, thin white fish fillets (such as john dory, snapper, bream, trevally or halibut), skin on**

PREPARATION 10 minutes

COOKING 10 minutes

SERVES 4

## Variation

The fish can be lightly dusted in seasoned plain (all-purpose) flour for a crisper texture; you can add flavourings such as ground cayenne pepper, fresh or dried parsley or garlic powder to the flour.

EACH SERVING PROVIDES
709 kJ, 169 kcal, 32 g protein, 2 g fat
(1 g saturated fat), 3 g carbohydrate
(3 g sugars), 2 g fibre, 161 mg sodium

1   Trim the ends from the asparagus. If the spears are thick, cut them in half lengthwise, then slice them in half diagonally. Cut the tomatoes in half. Rinse and drain the capers. Juice 1 lemon and cut the other into wedges.

2   Heat a large frying pan over medium–high heat. Make two diagonal slashes through the skin of each fish fillet and pat dry with paper towels. Sprinkle the fish with salt and freshly ground black pepper. Lightly oil the pan. When the oil is hot, add the fish, skin side down, and cook for 3–5 minutes, or until the skin is crisp and the flesh starts to turn white.

3   Turn the fish and add the asparagus, tomatoes, capers and lemon juice to the pan. Cook for a further 1–2 minutes, or until the fish is just cooked through.

4   Arrange the fish on a serving platter and pile the asparagus and tomato mixture over the top. Serve immediately, with the lemon wedges.

## Serving suggestion
Serve with steamed jasmine rice (Thai fragrant rice), steamed English spinach, broccoli or a mixture of green and yellow beans.

# Herbed tomato mussels with risoni

1½ cups (275 g) risoni (rice-shaped pasta)

2 brown (yellow) onions

3 x 410 g (15 oz) cans tomatoes with oregano and basil

¾ cup (130 g) black olives

1.5 kg (3 lb) mussels, shells cleaned and beards removed

PREPARATION 10 minutes

COOKING 15 minutes

SERVES 4

1  Bring a medium saucepan of water to a boil. Add the risoni and cook for 8–10 minutes, or according to the packet instructions, until al dente.

2  Meanwhile, slice the onions into thin wedges. Heat 1 tablespoon olive oil in a large saucepan over medium–high heat, add the onions and sauté for 3 minutes, or until softened. Add the tomatoes and olives and cook for a further 3 minutes, or until the mixture is hot and bubbling.

3  Add the mussels to the pan and cook for 5–6 minutes, or until the mussels open.

4  Drain the risoni and divide among four large bowls. Spoon the mussels and sauce over the risoni and serve immediately.

## Serving suggestion
Crumbled fetta goes beautifully with the mussels, melting into the sauce.

## Variations
- Add some chopped chilli and fresh basil or parsley.
- Use clams (vongole) or pipis in place of mussels.
- Instead of canned tomatoes, use tomato passata (puréed tomatoes), your favourite tomato pasta sauce, or 8 large tomatoes, diced and cooked with ½ cup (125 ml) red or white wine.
- Use spaghetti or soba noodles instead of risoni.

## Cook's tip
Before cooking, discard any mussels that are already open and that don't close when tapped. If any mussels don't open when cooked, remove them from the pan and prise them open with the tip of a knife. If they look like the other opened mussels and they smell of the sea, they are safe to eat. Your sense of smell will tell you if they are 'off'.

EACH SERVING PROVIDES
2804 kJ, 670 kcal, 51 g protein, 12 g fat (2 g saturated fat), 87 g carbohydrate (14 g sugars), 5 g fibre, 2931 mg sodium

seafood

# Cajun fish with salad

PREPARATION 5 minutes

COOKING 10 minutes

SERVES 4

## Cook's tip

You could also use a plate-sized whole fish (such as snapper, bream, blue-eye trevally or mackerel). Make 2–3 diagonal slashes through the thickest part of the flesh, rub the spice mix into the slashes and bake in a 200°C (400°F/Gas 6) oven for 12–15 minutes, or until cooked.

EACH SERVING PROVIDES
1074 kJ, 256 kcal, 34 g protein, 9 g fat (2 g saturated fat), 11 g carbohydrate (4 g sugars), 2 g fibre, 1427 mg sodium

4 firm white fish fillets, such as blue-eye trevalla, kingfish, haddock or pollock, about 150 g (5 oz) each
2 tablespoons Cajun spice mix (see Basics)
150 g (5 oz) mixed salad leaves
250 g (8 oz) cherry tomatoes
⅔ cup (115 g) black olives

1  Brush the fish fillets with a little extra virgin olive oil, then coat all over with the Cajun spice mix.

2  Wash the salad leaves and tomatoes and shake off the excess water. Cut the tomatoes in half, then gently toss in a bowl with the salad leaves and olives.

3  Heat a large frying pan over medium–high heat. Lightly brush the pan with olive oil and cook the fish for 4 minutes on each side, or until the flesh flakes easily when tested with a fork.

4  Serve the fish with the salad, drizzled with some extra virgin olive oil.

**Serving suggestion**
Drizzle the salad with a simple vinaigrette (see Basics).

## Variations

• You could bake the fish fillets in a 200°C (400°F/Gas 6) oven for 8–10 minutes, depending on their thickness.
• Rub the fish with another spice mix, such as piri piri or lemon pepper (see Basics).

# Teriyaki salmon with sweet potato

PREPARATION 10 minutes

COOKING 15 minutes

SERVES 4

## Cook's tip
The fish could also be grilled (broiled) or cooked on a barbecue.

EACH SERVING PROVIDES
1271 kJ, 304 kcal, 31 g protein, 11 g fat
(2 g saturated fat), 20 g carbohydrate
(11 g sugars), 2 g fibre, 179 mg sodium

1 tablespoon teriyaki sauce

1 tablespoon maple syrup

1 tablespoon wholegrain mustard

4 x 150 g (5 oz) salmon fillets, skin removed

350 g (12 oz) orange sweet potato

1　Preheat the oven to 220°C (425°F/Gas 7). Combine the teriyaki sauce, maple syrup and mustard in a flat dish. Place the salmon fillets in the marinade and turn to coat evenly.

2　Peel and thinly slice the orange sweet potato. Place in a large baking dish and toss with some olive oil, salt and freshly ground black pepper. Spread the slices out in a single layer and bake for 5 minutes.

3　Line a baking tray with baking (parchment) paper. Place the salmon on the baking tray, then drizzle the marinade from the dish over the sweet potatoes and lightly toss to coat. Transfer the salmon to the oven and bake with the sweet potatoes for 8–10 minutes, or until the salmon flakes easily when tested with a fork. Serve immediately.

### Serving suggestion
A simple green salad or some steamed broccolini or green beans are a lovely accompaniment.

## Variations
- Bake other vegetables with or instead of the sweet potato, such as potatoes, beetroot (beets), onions and fennel.
- Instead of baking the sweet potato, you could microwave or boil it until tender, then mash.

# Roasted fish with spice rub

2 tablespoons harissa or lemon pepper (see Basics), or your
  favourite spice mix
4 x 150 g (5 oz) firm-fleshed fish, such as ling, blue-eye trevalla,
  barramundi, pollock or haddock
200 g (7 oz) green beans
¾ cup (185 g) mayonnaise
2 teaspoons sumac

1  Preheat the oven to 200°C (400°F/Gas 6). Line a baking tray with
baking (parchment) paper. Mix the harissa with 1 tablespoon olive oil
and rub over each fish fillet. Place the fish on the baking tray and
bake for 8–10 minutes, or until cooked to your liking.

2  Meanwhile, top and tail the beans, then gently boil, steam or
microwave them for 3–4 minutes, or until just cooked.

3  In a small bowl, whisk the mayonnaise and sumac together.

4  Serve the fish with the beans and sumac mayonnaise.

## Variations

- Try this recipe using salmon fillets (leave the skin on if you wish).
- Add lemon or lime juice to the mayonnaise for added 'bite', or
substitute half the mayonnaise with yogurt.
- Instead of harissa, try piri piri or Cajun spice mix (see Basics).

PREPARATION 10 minutes

COOKING 10 minutes

SERVES 4

## Cook's tip

If you don't have sumac, use
½ teaspoon finely grated lemon
or lime zest, or 1 tablespoon
lemon or lime juice.

EACH SERVING PROVIDES
1478 kJ, 353 kcal, 33 g protein, 20 g fat
(3 g saturated fat), 11 g carbohydrate
(7 g sugars), 2 g fibre, 483 mg sodium

seafood

pasta, rice,
noodles & grains

# Top 10 pasta sauces

Pasta meals are always a big hit. While ready-made pasta sauces are convenient, it's so easy to cook up quick, luscious versions of your favourite sauces at home — just make our basic tomato or cream sauce and add any variation that takes your fancy.

## Super-easy tomato sauce

PREPARATION 5 minutes    COOKING 15 minutes    SERVES 4

1 onion
2 cloves garlic
2 x 410 g (15 oz) cans chopped tomatoes

Finely chop the onion. Heat 1 tablespoon olive oil in a saucepan over medium–low heat. Add the onion and cook for 4 minutes, or until soft. Crush the garlic into the pan and cook, stirring, for 1 minute. Stir in the tomatoes and sugar and bring to a boil. Reduce the heat to low and simmer for 5 minutes. Season to taste and serve over any type of pasta.

COOK'S TIP Adding a pinch of sugar balances the acid in the tomatoes. If you're serving this sauce plain, you can also add a good pinch of dried herbs such as basil or oregano. This recipe can also be halved, or you can freeze any leftover sauce in an airtight container for up to 2 months.

### Quick tricks to speed things up

● To cook pasta quickly, fill an electric kettle with water and bring to a boil. Pour the water into a large saucepan, cover and return to a boil over high heat. Stir a little salt into the water, and add 400 g (14 oz) dried pasta (to serve 4).

● Cover and return to a boil again. As soon as the water boils, remove the lid and cook that pasta over high heat according to packet directions, or until al dente. While the pasta is cooking, prepare the sauce.

● Fresh pasta only takes about 3 minutes to cook. In this case, get the water boiling but don't cook the pasta until the sauce is almost ready.

## Seafood marinara

When the tomato sauce has come to a boil, add 500 g (1 lb) **marinara mix**, or any prepared raw seafood such as prawns (shrimp), scallops, mussels, baby octopus, scallops and fish fillet pieces. Simmer for 5 minutes, or until the seafood is cooked through. Stir in 1 tablespoon chopped fresh **parsley**, season to taste and serve.

## Arrabiata

Add 1½ teaspoons **dried red chilli flakes** with the tomatoes. Just before serving, stir in 1 tablespoon chopped **parsley**.

## Puttanesca

Add 4 chopped **anchovy fillets** (canned anchovies) with the garlic; before seasoning, add 2 tablespoons chopped **pitted black olives**.

## Amatriciana

Add 100 g (3½ oz) chopped **bacon or pancetta** with the onion. Serve sprinkled with finely grated **pecorino cheese**.

## Bolognese

Add 400 g (14 oz) **minced (ground) beef** with the onion and cook over medium–high heat, breaking up any lumps with a wooden spoon. If desired, add 2 tablespoons **tomato paste (concentrated purée)** with the canned tomatoes.

# Simple creamy sauce

PREPARATION 5 minutes   COOKING 5 minutes   SERVES 4

**1 tablespoon butter**
**300 ml (10 fl oz) pouring (light) cream**
**⅔ cup (95 g) finely grated parmesan**

Drain the pasta into a large colander and set aside. Meanwhile, combine the butter, cream and parmesan in the pasta pot. Stir over medium heat until the cream is hot and the cheese has almost melted. Add the drained pasta and toss to coat in the sauce. Season to taste and serve.

## Boscaiola

While the pasta is cooking, chop 4 **rindless bacon slices (bacon strips)** and cook in the butter in a frying pan over medium heat for 4 minutes, or until lightly browned. Add 200 g (7 oz) sliced **button mushrooms** and cook for a further 2 minutes, or until soft. When the pasta is draining, scrape the bacon mixture into the pot and add the cream and parmesan. Add the drained pasta and toss to coat.

## Mornay

Add 2 teaspoons finely grated **lemon zest** to the cream mixture. Drain a 425 g (15 oz) **can tuna in oil** and flake with a fork. Add to the sauce with the pasta and toss to combine.

## Primavera

While the pasta is cooking, cut 175 g (6 oz) **asparagus** into 4 cm (1½ inch) lengths (if the spears are thick, cut each in half lengthwise first). Place in a heatproof bowl with 1 cup (150 g) **frozen peas** and cover with boiling water. Stand for 2 minutes, drain, then add to the sauce with the pasta.

## Herb

Add 4 tablespoons chopped fresh **chives** and 4 tablespoons chopped fresh **parsley** to the sauce with the pasta. (Also try other fresh herbs such as **dill** and **basil**.)

## Carbonara

While the pasta is cooking, chop 4 **rindless bacon slices (bacon strips)** and cook in the butter in a frying pan over medium heat for 4 minutes, or until lightly browned. Using a fork, whisk the cream and cheese with 3 **eggs**. When the pasta is draining, scrape the bacon mixture into the pot. Add the drained pasta, then pour the cream mixture over. Toss over medium heat for 2–3 minutes, or until the sauce thickens slightly as the egg sets.

# Ravioli with sweet potato

**500 g (1 lb) orange sweet potatoes**
**¼ cup (25 g) flaked almonds**
**20 fresh sage leaves**
**625 g (1 lb 4 oz) packet ricotta and spinach ravioli**
**⅓ cup (35 g) grated parmesan**

PREPARATION 10 minutes

COOKING 15 minutes

SERVES 4

## Quick tip

Don't cut the sweet potato into cubes any larger than 1 cm (½ inch), or they won't cook through properly.

EACH SERVING PROVIDES
2219 kJ, 530 kcal, 30 g protein, 15 g fat (6 g saturated fat), 70 g carbohydrate (9 g sugars), 5 g fibre, 115 mg sodium

1   Fill an electric kettle with water and bring to a boil. Peel the sweet potato and cut into small cubes.

2   Heat 2 tablespoons extra virgin olive oil in a large deep frying pan. Cook the sweet potato over medium heat for 12 minutes, or until tender and lightly browned, stirring occasionally. Add the almonds and sage and cook for a further 3 minutes, stirring often.

3   Meanwhile, pour the boiling water into a large saucepan, then cover and return to a boil over high heat. Season the water with a good pinch of salt and add the ravioli. Cover and return to a boil, then remove the lid and cook for 5 minutes. Drain well.

4   Add the ravioli to the frying pan. Drizzle with 1 tablespoon extra virgin olive oil, season with freshly ground black pepper and gently toss to combine. Divide among serving bowls, sprinkle with the parmesan and serve.

## Variations
- Use pumpkin (winter squash) instead of sweet potato.
- Experiment with different flavours of ravioli.

# Spaghetti vongole

PREPARATION 10 minutes

COOKING 10 minutes

SERVES 4

## Cook's tips

● To purge clams, cover them with salted water until ready to use. Drain and rinse the clams under running water, rubbing the shells against each other to remove any grit.

● Cooked clams can be removed from their shells by running a sharp knife under the flesh.

EACH SERVING PROVIDES
2291 kJ, 547 kcal, 45 g protein, 4 g fat
(<1 g saturated fat), 82 g carbohydrate
(<1 g sugars), <1 g fibre, 40 mg sodium

Purged clams, with the grit removed from their shells, are available from selected fishmongers, but if these aren't available it's easy to clean them at home.

**400 g (14 oz) spaghetti**

**1 kg (2 lb) small purged clams (vongole)**

**2 cloves garlic**

**2 teaspoons dried red chilli flakes**

**4 tablespoons chopped fresh flat-leaf parsley**

1 Fill an electric kettle with water and bring to a boil, then pour the water into a large saucepan. Cover and return to a boil over high heat. Season the water with a good pinch of salt and add the spaghetti. Cover and return to a boil, then cook, uncovered, for 8 minutes, or according to the packet instructions, until al dente.

2 Meanwhile, rinse the clams and set aside. Heat 2 tablespoons olive oil in a large deep frying pan. Crush the garlic into the oil, add the chilli flakes and cook over medium heat for 30 seconds. Add the clams, then cover and cook for 5 minutes. Discard any clams that haven't opened in this time.

3 Drain the spaghetti and add to the frying pan. Sprinkle with the parsley and toss to combine. Serve immediately.

### Serving suggestion
Offer some lemon wedges to squeeze over the pasta.

### Variations
● You can replace the clams with 1.5 kg (3 lb) mussels.
● If you have an open bottle of white wine, add a splash when you add the clams or mussels to the pan.

# Pasta with fetta & mint

## Shopping tip

Keep an eye out for a fetta that is marinated in olive oil; you can use the fetta and 1 tablespoon of the marinating oil in this recipe.

EACH SERVING PROVIDES
2008 kJ, 480 kcal, 22 g protein, 13 g fat (8 g saturated fat), 67 g carbohydrate (1 g sugars), 4 g fibre, 541 mg sodium

375 g (13 oz) fusilli or other spiral pasta

1¼ cups (195 g) frozen peas

1 small lemon

2 tablespoons chopped fresh mint leaves

200 g (7 oz) creamy fetta

1  Fill an electric kettle with water and bring to a boil, then pour the water into a large saucepan. Cover and return to a boil over high heat. Season the water with a good pinch of salt and add the pasta. Cover and return to a boil, then cook, uncovered, for 8 minutes. Add the peas, cover the pan again and return to a boil. Cook, uncovered, for a further 2 minutes, or until the pasta is al dente and the peas are cooked.

2  Meanwhile, zest and juice the lemon.

3  Drain the pasta and peas, then return them to the saucepan with the mint. Drizzle with 1 tablespoon extra virgin olive oil and season with freshly ground black pepper. Crumble the fetta over and toss to coat.

4  Divide the pasta among serving bowls and serve.

### Serving suggestion
Crumble some crisp cooked bacon or prosciutto over the top.

# Penne with tuna

375 g (13 oz) penne or other short pasta
150 g (5 oz) green beans
1 small red onion
200 g (7 oz) cherry tomatoes
185 g (6½ oz) can tuna in oil

PREPARATION 10 minutes

COOKING 15 minutes

SERVES 4

## Quick tip

To trim and halve the beans, line them up on a chopping board, slice the ends off in one go, then cut the beans in half.

EACH SERVING PROVIDES
1962 kJ, 469 kcal, 19 g protein, 14 g fat (2 g saturated fat), 66 g carbohydrate (2 g sugars), 5 g fibre, 157 mg sodium

1 Fill an electric kettle with water and bring to a boil, then pour the water into a large saucepan. Cover and return to a boil over high heat. Season the water with a good pinch of salt and add the pasta. Cover and return to a boil, then cook, uncovered, for 8 minutes. Meanwhile, trim the beans and cut them in half. Add the beans to the pan, then cover and return to a boil. Cook, uncovered, for a further 2 minutes, or until the pasta is al dente and the beans are cooked.

2 Meanwhile, halve and finely slice the onion, and cut the cherry tomatoes in half. Drain the tuna and flake the flesh with a fork.

3 Drain the pasta and beans, then return them to the saucepan. Drizzle with 1 tablespoon extra virgin olive oil and add the onion, tomatoes and tuna. Season with freshly ground black pepper, gently toss together and serve.

**Serving suggestion**
Serve with a crisp green salad and garlic bread.

pasta, rice, noodles & grains

# Gnocchi with creamy blue cheese sauce

PREPARATION 10 minutes

COOKING 10 minutes

SERVES 4

## Quick tip

When cooking pasta, using your electric kettle will reduce the time spent waiting for water to come to a boil.

EACH SERVING PROVIDES
1952 kJ, 466 kcal, 12 g protein, 23 g fat
(11 g saturated fat), 52 g carbohydrate
(2 g sugars), <1 g fibre, 287 mg sodium

⅔ cup (150 ml) pouring (light) cream
100 g (3½ oz) blue cheese
2 tablespoons chopped fresh chives
⅓ cup (40 g) walnut pieces
500 g (1 lb) fresh gnocchi

1   Fill an electric kettle with water and bring to a boil, then pour the water into a large saucepan. Cover and return to a boil over high heat.

2   Meanwhile, pour the cream into a saucepan and bring to a gentle simmer over low heat. Crumble or roughly chop the cheese, then add to the cream with most of the chives, reserving about 2 teaspoons for garnishing. Stir over low heat for 2 minutes, or until the cheese has melted. Stir in the walnuts.

3   While the sauce is cooking, add the gnocchi to the saucepan of boiling water and stir well. When the water comes to a boil again and the gnocchi are floating on the surface, drain the gnocchi.

4   Add the gnocchi to the sauce; mix gently and spoon into serving bowls. Sprinkle with the reserved chives and serve.

**Serving suggestion**
Serve with a green salad for a main course meal.

## Variations

- For a mild flavour, use a creamy blue cheese. The firmer blue cheeses will give a stronger 'blue' flavour.
- Use parmesan instead of blue cheese if you prefer.
- Some chopped fresh parsley adds a lovely flavour to the sauce.

pasta, rice, noodles & grains

# Vegetarian tortellini bake

**625 g (1 lb 4 oz) ricotta-filled tortellini**
**100 g (3½ oz) mushrooms**
**500 g (1 lb) jar tomato pasta sauce**
**1 cup (45 g) baby spinach leaves**
**1 cup (150 g) grated mozzarella**

1   Preheat the oven to 210°C (415°F/Gas 6–7). Meanwhile, fill an electric kettle with water and bring to a boil.

2   Pour the boiling water into a large saucepan, then cover and return to a boil over high heat. Season the water with a good pinch of salt and add the pasta. Cover and return to a boil, then remove the lid and cook for 5 minutes.

3   Meanwhile, slice the mushrooms. Drain the pasta well, then return to the pan and mix the pasta sauce, spinach and mushrooms through.

4   Spread the mixture into a baking dish measuring about 20 x 30 cm (8 x 12 inches) across, and 6 cm (2½ inches) deep. Sprinkle with the mozzarella and bake for 10 minutes, or until the cheese is golden brown and bubbling on top.

**Serving suggestion**
This pasta bake is lovely with a crisp green salad.

## Variation

Tortellini is available with many other delicious fillings — use any variety you like here.

PREPARATION 10 minutes

COOKING 15 minutes

SERVES 4

## Shortcut ingredients

To save on preparation time, buy pre-sliced mushrooms and pre-grated mozzarella.

EACH SERVING PROVIDES
1433 kJ, 342 kcal, 21 g protein, 17 g fat
(10 g saturated fat), 26 g carbohydrate
(13 g sugars), 5 g fibre, 1169 mg sodium

pasta, rice, noodles & grains

# Easy asparagus & broccoli risotto

A traditional risotto is stirred constantly during cooking, while the hot stock is gradually being added. This version is so much simpler — and virtually hands-free.

1½ cups (330 g) arborio rice

2 vegetable stock (bouillon) cubes

1 large head of broccoli, about 400 g (14 oz)

12 thin asparagus spears

½ cup (50 g) grated parmesan or Grana Padano cheese

1 Bring 4 cups (1 litre) water to a boil in an electric kettle; pour into a large saucepan. Add the rice and crumbled stock cubes, cover and bring to a boil over high heat. Remove the lid, stir briefly, then reduce heat to medium–low. Put the lid back on, tilted slightly, and cook for 10 minutes, stirring occasionally.

2 Meanwhile, trim the stalk from the broccoli, then cut the head into small florets. Trim the asparagus spears and cut diagonally into 3 cm (1¼ inch) lengths.

3 Stir the broccoli and asparagus through the rice. Increase the heat to medium and cook, covered tightly, for a further 4–5 minutes — the rice should be a soft consistency.

4 Remove the risotto from the heat. Season with freshly ground black pepper; stir in the parmesan and 1 tablespoon extra virgin olive oil. Cover and allow to stand for 5 minutes before serving.

**Serving suggestion**
Serve the risotto with a salad for a balanced meal.

## Variations

- You can use 50 g (1¾ oz) blue cheese instead of parmesan.
- Before serving, stir some hot shredded barbecued chicken through the risotto.

PREPARATION 10 minutes

COOKING 15 minutes

SERVES 4

## Shopping tips

- Buy good Italian arborio rice for this recipe. The short, plump, starchy grains hold their shape and absorb flavours well.
- If you would like this recipe to be gluten-free, look for gluten-free stock cubes in your supermarket.

EACH SERVING PROVIDES
1553 kJ, 371 kcal, 15 g protein, 4 g fat (3 g saturated fat), 66 g carbohydrate (1 g sugars), 5 g fibre, 478 mg sodium

pasta, rice, noodles & grains

225

# Simple fried rice

## Shortcut ingredients

Instead of using cooked rice, you can buy pre-cooked rice in pouches at the supermarket. You can use it straight from the pouch for this recipe, as the rice is already fully cooked and only needs heating.

EACH SERVING PROVIDES
1377 kJ, 329 kcal, 22 g protein, 5 g fat
(1 g saturated fat), 50 g carbohydrate
(1 g sugars), 1 g fibre, 816 mg sodium

For this recipe use leftover rice, or cook 1 cup (220 g) raw rice a day ahead — this ensures your fried rice will be dry and fluffy, not gluggy. Refrigerate the cooked rice until needed.

**3 eggs**

**4 spring onions (scallions)**

**250 g (8 oz) small peeled prawns (shrimp)**

**5½ cups (650 g) cooked and cooled jasmine rice (Thai fragrant rice)**

**2 tablespoons soy sauce, or to taste**

1  Using a fork, whisk the eggs in a small bowl. Heat 2 teaspoons vegetable oil in a wok or large deep frying pan over medium–high heat. Pour in the eggs and swirl them around the base of the wok to make a thin omelette. Cook for 2 minutes, or until set and lightly golden underneath, then turn and cook the other side for 1 minute — don't worry if the omelette breaks up when you try to turn it. Remove from the pan and cool slightly, then roll the omelette up and cut into slices.

2  Finely slice the spring onions and set aside. Wipe the wok out if necessary and heat another 2 teaspoons oil in the wok. Add the prawns and stir-fry for 3 minutes, or until they change colour. Add most of the the spring onions, reserving some as a garnish, and stir-fry for 1 minute.

3  Fold the rice through and cook for a further minute or two, until combined and heated through.

4  Add the egg, drizzle the soy sauce over, then fold through until combined. Serve garnished with the remaining spring onions.

### Serving suggestion
Round the dish out by serving it with stir-fried Asian greens such as choy sum or gai lan.

# Easy tuna pilaf

PREPARATION 10 minutes

COOKING 15 minutes

SERVES 4

## Cook's tip

For a more traditional pilaf, add a pinch of saffron or turmeric to the rice. Toss some toasted flaked almonds or pistachios through the rice before serving, along with some currants or raisins.

EACH SERVING PROVIDES
1413 kJ, 338 kcal, 25 g protein, 2 g fat (1 g saturated fat), 52 g carbohydrate (2 g sugars), 1 g fibre, 612 mg sodium

**1 onion**

**1¼ cups (250 g) basmati rice**

**3 teaspoons good chicken or vegetable stock (bouillon) powder**

**1 cup (130 g) frozen baby peas**

**2 x 185 g (6½ oz) cans lemon-infused tuna**

1   Bring 2½ cups (625 ml) water to a boil in an electric kettle. Meanwhile, heat 1 tablespoon olive oil in a large, heavy-based saucepan. Chop the onion, add to the pan and cook over medium–high heat for 3 minutes, or until softened. Add the rice and stir to coat in the oil.

2   Stir the boiling water into the rice with the stock powder. Cover and bring to a boil. Reduce the heat to medium–low and cook, tightly covered, for 7 minutes. Uncover very briefly, scatter the peas on top, then cover and cook for a further 5 minutes. Turn off the heat and allow the rice to stand for 5 minutes.

3   Meanwhile, drain and flake the tuna. Remove the pan from the heat and gently fold the peas and tuna through. Serve immediately.

**Serving suggestion**
A tomato, olive and red onion salad goes well with this dish.

## Variation

Canned tuna is available these days with many different flavourings added. Try tuna infused with chilli or sun-dried tomatoes, or your favourite flavour combination.

# Spiced rice pulao

**2 cloves garlic**
**2 teaspoons Moroccan spice mix (see Basics)**
**1 cup (220 g) basmati rice**
**420 g (15 oz) can chickpeas**
**100 g (3½ oz) baby spinach leaves**

PREPARATION 10 minutes

COOKING 15 minutes

SERVES 4 as a side dish

## Cook's tip

Moroccan spice mix is a popular mixture of dry ground spices. It is available from the supermarket, or you can make your own using our recipe in the Basics chapter. You can substitute any spice mixture for a different flavour.

EACH SERVING PROVIDES
1106 kJ, 264 kcal, 9 g protein, 2 g fat (<1 g saturated fat), 52 g carbohydrate (1 g sugars), 4 g fibre, 170 mg sodium

1   Bring 2 cups (500 ml) water to a boil in an electric kettle. Meanwhile, pour 1½ tablespoons olive oil into a large heavy-based saucepan. Crush the garlic into the oil and add the spice mix. Place the pan over medium–low heat, and when the oil starts to sizzle, stir for about 30 seconds. Add the rice and stir for about 1½ minutes to coat the rice in the flavoured oil and lightly toast it.

2   Add the boiling water to the pan with a good pinch of salt; stir briefly. Cover and bring to a boil over high heat. Reduce the heat to medium–low and cook, tightly covered, for 10 minutes.

3   Drain and rinse the chickpeas; drain again. Uncover the pan very briefly and stir the chickpeas and spinach through the rice. Cover and cook for a further 3 minutes.

4   Remove from the heat and allow to stand for 5 minutes before serving.

## Serving suggestion

This pulao makes a simple vegetarian meal, or a lovely side dish to meat. Serve with a salad of tomatoes, finely sliced red onion and coriander (cilantro) leaves.

pasta, rice, noodles & grains

# Mee goreng

PREPARATION 10 minutes

COOKING 10 minutes

SERVES 4

## Cook's tips

Use white or red cabbage, or even a combination of both.

EACH SERVING PROVIDES
1380 kJ, 330 kcal, 26 g protein, 8 g fat
(2 g saturated fat), 37 g carbohydrate
(2 g sugars), 3 g fibre, 768 mg sodium

**200 g (7 oz) dry egg noodles**

**400 g (14 oz) boneless, skinless chicken thighs**

**200 g (7 oz) cabbage**

**3 spring onions (scallions)**

**2 tablespoons soy sauce**

1  Fill an electric kettle with water and bring to a boil, then pour the water into a saucepan. Cover and bring to a boil over high heat. Add the noodles and cook for 4 minutes, or according to the packet instructions, until tender. Drain well.

2  Meanwhile, cut the chicken into 2 cm (¾ inch) pieces. Roughly chop the cabbage; finely slice the spring onions. Heat 2 teaspoons vegetable oil in a large wok or deep frying pan over high heat. Working in two batches, add the chicken and stir-fry for 3 minutes, or until golden brown and cooked through. Transfer to a bowl.

3  Heat another 2 teaspoons oil in the wok and add the cabbage and spring onions. Stir-fry over medium–high heat for 2 minutes, or until just softened.

4  Add the noodles and soy sauce to the wok, along with the chicken. Toss to combine and briefly heat through. Serve immediately.

**Serving suggestion**
Offer some extra soy sauce and sweet chilli sauce on the side.

# Red curry noodles

300 g (10 oz) rice vermicelli noodles
500 g (1 lb) firm tofu
2 tablespoons red curry paste
400 ml (14 fl oz) can coconut milk
500 g (1 lb) packet frozen mixed stir-fry vegetables

1  Fill an electric kettle with water and bring to a boil. Place the noodles in a large heatproof bowl, cover with boiling water and allow to soften for 8 minutes. Meanwhile, cut the tofu into 2 cm (¾ inch) cubes and pat dry with paper towels.

2  Heat 2 tablespoons vegetable oil in a large wok or deep frying pan over high heat. Add the tofu and stir-fry for 2 minutes, or until crisp and lightly golden. Using a slotted spoon or spatula, transfer to a plate.

3  Add the curry paste to the wok and cook over medium heat for 1 minute. Stir in the coconut milk and add the vegetables. Cover and bring to a boil, then remove the lid and cook for 5 minutes, or until the vegetables are hot. Stir in the tofu.

4  Drain the noodles and divide among serving bowls. Top with the tofu and vegetables, ladle the curry sauce over and serve.

PREPARATION 10 minutes

COOKING 10 minutes

SERVES 4

## Shopping tip
If possible, choose a Thai-style stir-fry vegetable mix for this dish. If fresh limes are available, buy one to squeeze over the dish.

EACH SERVING PROVIDES
2892 kJ, 691 kcal, 22 g protein, 31 g fat (20 g saturated fat), 77 g carbohydrate (8 g sugars), 9 g fibre, 190 mg sodium

pasta, rice, noodles & grains

233

# Quick pad Thai

**375 g (13 oz) rice stick noodles**

**200 g (7 oz) bean sprouts**

**3 eggs**

**240 g (8 oz) jar pad Thai paste**

**½ cup (25 g) roughly chopped fresh coriander (cilantro),
plus extra to garnish**

PREPARATION 10 minutes

COOKING 5 minutes

SERVES 4

## Cook's tip

Rice stick noodles are flat, dried noodles, which come in different widths. Pad Thai pastes vary in heat, so check the instructions on the jar for the right amount to use.

EACH SERVING PROVIDES
2376 kJ, 567 kcal, 10 g protein, 7 g fat
(2 g saturated fat), 111 g carbohydrate
(14 g sugars), 3 g fibre, 2173 mg sodium

1   Fill an electric kettle with water and bring to a boil. Place the noodles in a large heatproof bowl, cover with boiling water and leave to soften for 10 minutes. Meanwhile, trim any scraggly tails from the bean sprouts.

2   When the noodles are nearly soft, lightly whisk the eggs with a fork. Heat 2 teaspoons vegetable oil in a wok over medium–high heat, then pour in the eggs and swirl them around the base of the wok to make a thin omelette. Cook for 1 minute, then remove from the pan and cool slightly. Roll the omelette up and cut into slices.

3   Add the pad Thai paste to the wok and stir-fry over medium heat for 1 minute. Drain the noodles, then add them to the wok with the bean sprouts. Toss to coat the noodles and to soften the sprouts slightly.

4   Toss the egg and coriander through the noodles. Serve sprinkled with extra coriander.

## Serving suggestion
Authentic garnishes for pad Thai include chopped roasted unsalted peanuts, lime wedges, crispy fried Asian shallots, chopped Thai basil and cooked prawns (shrimp).

# Chicken satay noodles

PREPARATION 10 minutes

COOKING 10 minutes

SERVES 4

## Shopping tip

Look for fresh hokkien noodles in the refrigerator section of the supermarket or Asian food stores.

## Cook's tip

Satay sauce may come in a different can or jar size where you live, so check the label and adjust the quantity as needed. To make your own satay sauce, see Basics.

EACH SERVING PROVIDES
2006 kJ, 479 kcal, 25 g protein, 20 g fat
(6 g saturated fat), 48 g carbohydrate
(12 g sugars), 3 g fibre, 591 mg sodium

**450 g (1 lb) fresh thin hokkien (egg) noodles**

**150 g (5 oz) snow peas (mangetout)**

**1 large carrot**

**300 g (10 oz) boneless, skinless chicken breast**

**250 g (8 oz) can satay sauce**

1   Fill an electric kettle with water and bring to a boil. Place the noodles in a large heatproof bowl and cover with boiling water. Allow to soften for 2 minutes, then use a chopstick or fork to loosen the noodles. Drain into a colander and set aside.

2   Meanwhile, trim the tops from the snow peas, then cut into thin slices diagonally. Thinly slice the carrot. Cut the chicken into 2 cm (¾ inch) pieces.

3   Heat 2 teaspoons vegetable oil in a large wok or deep frying pan over high heat. Working in two batches, cook the chicken for 3 minutes and transfer to a plate.

4   Reduce the heat to medium–high and heat another 2 teaspoons oil in the wok. Add the carrot and stir-fry for 1 minute. Add the snow peas and stir-fry for 1 minute. Add the chicken, noodles and satay sauce and toss for a further minute or two, until combined and heated through. Serve immediately.

## Variations

- Instead of chicken, use thinly sliced pork fillet.
- Use a different type of noodle if you like.

# Soba noodles with salmon & avocado

**270 g (9½ oz) packet soba noodles**
**2 x 250 g (8 oz) salmon fillets, skin removed**
**4 spring onions (scallions)**
**1 avocado**
**2 tablespoons ponzu sauce (see Basics)**

PREPARATION 10 minutes

COOKING 10 minutes

SERVES 4

## Cook's tip

Ponzu sauce is a Japanese sauce used for dipping or dressing. It is available from large supermarkets and specialty food shops. If you can't find it, substitute soy sauce mixed with lemon juice.

EACH SERVING PROVIDES
2363 kJ, 564 kcal, 34 g protein, 24 g fat (5 g saturated fat), 52 g carbohydrate (2 g sugars), 3 g fibre, 789 mg sodium

1   Fill an electric kettle with water and bring to a boil, then pour the water into a saucepan. Cover and return to a boil over high heat. Add the noodles, cover and bring back to a boil, then remove the lid and cook for 4 minutes, or until tender. Drain the noodles into a colander, then rinse under cold running water. Set aside to drain.

2   Meanwhile, heat 2 teaspoons vegetable oil in a non-stick frying pan over medium heat. Add the salmon and cook for 3 minutes on each side, or until just cooked through. Allow to cool slightly, then flake into chunks.

3   While the salmon and noodles are cooking, finely slice the spring onions and dice the avocado flesh.

4   Place the noodles in a large bowl and drizzle with the ponzu sauce. Add the spring onions, salmon and avocado and gently toss to combine. Serve immediately.

### Serving suggestion
These noodles are meant to be served cold, and make a lovely meal for a hot day. Sprinkle with toasted sesame seeds if desired.

pasta, rice, noodles & grains

# Couscous with haloumi

PREPARATION 10 minutes

COOKING 5 minutes

SERVES 4

## Cook's tip

Haloumi is a salty cheese with a firm texture. Eat it hot from the pan, as it can become rubbery on cooling. If you can't find haloumi, crumble some fetta cheese over the couscous instead.

EACH SERVING PROVIDES
1301 kJ, 310 kcal, 18 g protein, 9 g fat (5 g saturated fat), 38 g carbohydrate (3 g sugars), 1 g fibre, 1866 mg sodium

1¼ cups (310 ml) chicken or vegetable stock
1 cup (185 g) instant couscous
200 g (7 oz) haloumi cheese
200 g (7 oz) cherry tomatoes
1¼ cups (50 g) baby rocket (arugula) leaves

1 Pour the stock into a saucepan, then cover and return to a boil over high heat. Turn off the heat, uncover briefly and add the couscous. Quickly put the lid back on and swirl the pan to submerge the couscous. Stand for 5 minutes, then remove the lid. Drizzle with 1 tablespoon olive oil and fluff up the grains with a fork. Transfer to a large bowl.

2 Meanwhile, cut the haloumi into slices about 7 mm (³⁄₈ inch) thick, and cut the tomatoes in half. Heat 2 teaspoons olive oil in a large non-stick frying pan over medium–high heat. Add the haloumi and cook for 30–60 seconds on each side, or until golden brown.

3 Mix the tomatoes and rocket through the couscous. Divide among serving plates, top with the hot haloumi slices and serve.

**Serving suggestion**
Serve with lemon wedges to squeeze over the haloumi.

# Quick burghul salad with lamb

1 cup (175 g) burghul (bulgur)

4 spring onions (scallions)

2 large tomatoes

1 tablespoon lemon juice

12 frenched lamb cutlets

PREPARATION 10 minutes

COOKING 5 minutes

SERVES 4

1   Bring 1¼ cups (310 ml) water to a boil in an electric kettle. Place the burghul in a heatproof bowl and pour the boiling water over. Cover tightly with foil and allow to stand for 12 minutes, or until the grains are tender. Meanwhile, finely slice the spring onions, and chop the tomatoes.

2   Place the burghul in a large salad bowl and add the lemon juice, spring onions and tomatoes. Drizzle with 1 tablespoon extra virgin olive oil, season to taste with salt and freshly ground black pepper and toss to combine.

3   Meanwhile, lightly oil a chargrill pan and heat to medium–high. Cook the lamb cutlets for 2 minutes on each side for medium. Serve with the burghul salad.

### Serving suggestion
Sprinkle the salad with chopped fresh parsley or coriander (cilantro).

## Shopping tip

Ask your butcher for Frenched lamb cutlets. These have been trimmed of fat, with the bone scraped clean for a nicer look.

EACH SERVING PROVIDES
1445 kJ, 345 kcal, 32 g protein, 13 g fat (5 g saturated fat), 28 g carbohydrate (3 g sugars), 9 g fibre, 92 mg sodium

*pasta, rice, noodles & grains*

# Polenta with mushrooms & broccolini

PREPARATION 10 minutes

COOKING 10 minutes

SERVES 4

## Cook's tip

Instant polenta has a slightly finer texture than regular polenta, allowing it to cook more quickly. To avoid lumps forming, stir it in one direction only.

EACH SERVING PROVIDES
1775 kJ, 424 kcal, 20 g protein, 9 g fat (4 g saturated fat), 65 g carbohydrate (10 g sugars), 5 g fibre, 2355 mg sodium

**6 cups (1.5 litres) vegetable stock**

**75 g (2½ oz) parmesan**

**1½ cups (285 g) instant, coarse-grain polenta**

**400 g (14 oz) broccolini**

**250 g (8 oz) fresh mixed mushrooms, such as shiitake, Swiss brown or button mushrooms**

1  Pour the stock into a large saucepan and bring to a boil. Meanwhile, using a vegetable peeler, shave some of the parmesan into flakes and save for garnishing; grate the remaining parmesan. Reduce the heat to medium and gradually sprinkle the polenta into the stock, stirring occasionally with a wooden spoon to prevent lumps forming. Remove from the heat and stir in the grated parmesan.

2  Meanwhile, half-fill an electric kettle with water and bring to a boil, then pour the water into a saucepan and return to a boil. Trim the stem end of the broccolini, and cut the stalks in half if preferred. Cook for 3–4 minutes, or until just tender. Drain.

3  Wipe the mushrooms clean with a damp cloth, then trim the stems and slice the caps. Heat 1 tablespoon olive oil in a large frying pan over medium–high heat. Add the mushrooms and sauté for 3–4 minutes, or until tender.

4  Spoon the polenta onto serving plates. Top with the mushrooms and broccolini, sprinkle with the reserved parmesan flakes and serve.

## Variations

- Use asparagus instead of broccolini.
- Stir baby spinach leaves or chopped fresh herbs, such as parsley, coriander (cilantro) or chives, into the hot polenta.
- For a creamier consistency, substitute half the stock with milk.
- For a richer taste, stir some chopped butter through the hot polenta.

pasta, rice, noodles & grains

# Buckwheat & cranberry salad

This taste-tingling salad is great at a barbecue, or as an accompaniment to any meat or chicken dish.

**1 cup (190 g) roasted buckwheat**

**2 tablespoons shelled pistachios**

**⅔ cup (80 g) dried cranberries**

**¼ cup (60 ml) lemon juice**

**3 tablespoons chopped fresh flat-leaf parsley**

1   Preheat the oven to 180°C (350°C/Gas 4). Pour 1½ cups (375 ml) water into a saucepan, then cover and return to a boil over high heat. Reduce the heat to low, quickly add the buckwheat and replace the lid. Simmer gently for 10 minutes, then turn off the heat.

2   Meanwhile, spread the pistachios on a baking tray and bake for 3–5 minutes, or until lightly toasted. Cool slightly and roughly chop.

3   Uncover the saucepan briefly and mix the cranberries through the buckwheat. Put the lid back on and allow to stand for 5 minutes.

4   Transfer the buckwheat mixture to a large bowl and allow to cool slightly, stirring occasionally to release the heat. Add 1 tablespoon extra virgin olive oil, the lemon juice, parsley and pistachios. Mix together until well combined and serve.

PREPARATION 10 minutes

COOKING 15 minutes

SERVES 4

## Cook's tip

High in protein and nutrients, buckwheat isn't actually a variety of wheat at all, and is gluten-free. Roasted buckwheat (sometimes known as 'kasha') has a nuttier flavour than ordinary buckwheat. You'll find buckwheat in health food stores and the health food aisle of larger supermarkets.

EACH SERVING PROVIDES
1192 kJ, 284 kcal, 7 g protein, 5 g fat (1 g saturated fat), 52 g carbohydrate (14 g sugars), 3 g fibre, 8 mg sodium

pasta, rice, noodles & grains

vegetables

# Love those vegetables!

The kaleidoscope of tastes, colours, shapes and textures of vegetables can make an otherwise ordinary meal so much more appealing. Celebrate the seasons and enjoy the nutritional benefits the mighty vegetable kingdom has to offer.

## Dressed for success

It's so easy to 'dress up' cooked vegetables with a simple sauce. Here's a handful of classic sauces that will complement a huge range of vegetables.

### Creamy white sauce

Melt 50 g (1¾ oz) unsalted butter in a saucepan. Add 1 crushed garlic clove and cook, stirring, over medium–low heat for 1 minute. Add 1½ tablespoons plain (all-purpose) flour and cook for 2 minutes, stirring constantly. Gradually pour in 1¼ cups (310 ml) milk and stir for 3 minutes, or until smooth and thickened. Stir in ½ cup (125 g) sour cream, natural (plain) yogurt or cream and 1½ tablespoons dijon mustard. Season to taste and serve.

**OPTIONAL EXTRAS** Add sliced mushrooms, spring onions (scallions), grated cheddar or parmesan and fresh or dried herbs, such as parsley and chives.

### Fresh tomato sauce

Heat 1 tablespoon olive oil in a saucepan. Add 2 chopped onions and 2 crushed garlic cloves and cook for about 5 minutes over medium heat. Stir in two 410 g (15 oz) cans of whole tomatoes (or tomatoes with herbs) and simmer for 5 minutes, or until thickened. Season to taste and serve.

**OPTIONAL EXTRAS** Add chopped fresh or dried herbs, and a dash of worcestershire sauce, chilli sauce, Tabasco sauce or sambal oelek. For a chunky sauce add diced capsicums (bell peppers), celery and black olives.

### Roasted capsicum sauce

Preheat the oven to 200°C (400°F/Gas 6). Remove the stem, seeds and membranes from a red capsicum (bell pepper), then place on a baking tray lined with baking (parchment) paper, cut side down. Roast for 15–20 minutes, or until the skin is blistered and charred. Place in a plastic bag and set aside for 10 minutes (the steam helps to lift off the skin). Remove the skin and purée the flesh with a little olive oil to your preferred consistency. Season to taste and serve.

**OPTIONAL EXTRAS** Add chopped olives, capers and thyme.

### Balsamic glaze

In a small saucepan, combine ⅔ cup (150 ml) balsamic vinegar, ½ cup (100 g) soft brown sugar and ½ cup (125 ml) water. Simmer for 5–6 minutes over medium heat, or until thickened slightly. Season to taste and serve.

### Tahini miso sauce

Whisk together 2 tablespoons tahini, 2 tablespoons white miso paste, 3 tablespoons olive oil, ⅓ cup (80 ml) water and 1 tablespoon lemon juice and drizzle over vegetables.

### Cook's tip

● Caramelised onion is a quick, delicious side dish to so many dishes. Heat 1 tablespoon olive oil in a pan over medium heat. Add 1 sliced onion and cook for 5 minutes. Add 2 tablespoons balsamic vinegar and 1 tablespoon soft brown sugar and season to taste. Cook for 5 minutes, or until caramelised.

# To top it off

Add some texture to vegetables with a crunchy topping. Here's just a few ideas to get you started.

## Toasted nuts or sesame seeds

Preheat the oven to 180°C (350°F/Gas 4). Spread some nuts or sesame seeds on a baking tray lined with baking (parchment) paper and bake for 5–10 minutes, or until golden. Alternatively, fry them in a dry frying pan over medium heat for 5–10 minutes, or until golden, stirring them so they don't burn. Sprinkle over cooked vegetables.

## Fresh breadcrumbs

Here's a great way to use up leftover bread! Remove the crusts from day-old white bread slices, cut the bread into cubes and process in a food processor until finely chopped. Seal in a plastic bag and refrigerate or freeze for up to 3 months. Use the crumbs to coat sliced vegetables such as eggplant (aubergine), before pan-frying or baking them.

## Toasted breadcrumbs

Toss some breadcrumbs with a little olive oil in a frying pan over medium heat for 3–5 minutes, or until crunchy, stirring continuously. Sprinkle over cooked vegetables.

**OPTIONAL EXTRAS** Add grated cheddar or parmesan; chopped black or green olives; capers or sun-dried tomatoes; toasted sesame seeds; fresh or dried herbs such as parsley, basil, rosemary, dill, oregano or thyme; add spices such as ground cumin, paprika or cayenne pepper.

## Pesto, pesto, pesto!

Top your favourite vegetables with a nutty dollop of basil pesto (see Basics), but also experiment with the delicious pesto variations given below.

**VARIATIONS** Instead of basil use mint, parsley or rocket (arugula); toast the pine nuts for extra flavour; instead of pine nuts, use other nuts such as cashews, almonds or macadamias; add 1 teaspoon white vinegar or lemon juice for extra 'zing'.

# Quick vegetable 'lasagne'

**PREPARATION** 10 minutes

**COOKING** 15 minutes

**SERVES** 4

## Shortcut ingredients

To save time, buy pre-grated parmesan; you'll only need about ³⁄₄ cup. You can also often buy chargrilled eggplant from the deli.

## Cook's tip

You can use frozen spinach instead of fresh spinach. Thaw it first, then squeeze out all the excess liquid before using.

EACH SERVING PROVIDES
1486 kJ, 355 kcal, 24 g protein, 21 g fat
(13 g saturated fat), 12 g carbohydrate
(10 g sugars), 4 g fibre, 548 mg sodium

**2 eggplants (aubergines), about 500 g (1 lb) in total**
**250 g (8 oz) baby spinach leaves**
**500 g (1 lb) ricotta**
**75 g (2½ oz) parmesan**
**2 cups (500 ml) good-quality pasta sauce**

1  Preheat the oven to 230°C (450°F/Gas 8). Line a large baking tray with baking (parchment) paper. Cut the eggplants into 1 cm (½ inch) slices, leaving the skin on. Lightly spray or brush both sides with olive or vegetable oil, spread the slices on the baking tray and bake for 10 minutes.

2  Meanwhile, put the spinach in a heatproof bowl and pour some boiling water over. Leave to wilt for 1 minute, then drain and squeeze out any excess liquid. Chop the spinach finely and place in a dry bowl with the ricotta. Season with salt and freshly ground black pepper and mix to combine.

3  Spread the mixture over each eggplant slice and bake for a further 5 minutes. Meanwhile, grate the parmesan, and warm the pasta sauce in a saucepan over medium heat.

4  Place an eggplant ricotta slice on each plate. Drizzle with the pasta sauce and parmesan. Repeat with another eggplant slice and drizzle with more pasta sauce. Sprinkle with the remaining parmesan and serve immediately.

## Variations
● Substitute or add other vegetables, such as chargrilled zucchini (courgettes) and capsicums (bell peppers).
● Instead of parmesan, use fetta.

vegetables

# Green vegetable toss

1 large brown (yellow) onion
250 g (8 oz) green beans
250 g (8 oz) sugarsnap peas
250 g (8 oz) broccolini
¾ cup (180 ml) vegetable stock

1  Slice the onion into wedges. Trim the beans and peas. Cut the broccolini stalks in half crosswise, then slice into thinner florets.

2  Heat 1 tablespoon peanut oil in a wok or large frying pan over medium–high heat. Add the onion and cook for 2 minutes, tossing occasionally. Add the beans, peas and stock and simmer for 3 minutes, tossing occasionally.

3  Add the broccolini and simmer for a further 2–4 minutes, or until the vegetables are just cooked. Serve immediately.

### Serving suggestion
Serve with steamed rice and soy sauce, or cooked pasta, such as penne.

## Variations
- Garnish with roasted almonds or roasted sesame seeds, or drizzle with sesame oil.
- Add some grated fresh ginger for extra 'zing'.
- For a vegetarian meal, add some seasoned diced tofu.

PREPARATION 10 minutes

COOKING 10 minutes

SERVES 4

## Shopping tip
Depending on what vegetables happen to be in season, you can add or substitute other chopped fresh vegetables, such as green capsicum (bell pepper), celery, asparagus, Asian greens and/or broccoli.

EACH SERVING PROVIDES
330 kJ, 78 kcal, 6 g protein, <1 g fat (<1 g saturated fat), 12 g carbohydrate (7 g sugars), 4 g fibre, 273 mg sodium

# Baked stuffed mushrooms

PREPARATION 5 minutes

COOKING 15 minutes

SERVES 4

## Cook's tip

To make fresh breadcrumbs, cut the crusts off sliced bread. Put the bread in a food processor and briefly pulse until chopped to your preferred consistency.

EACH SERVING PROVIDES
1316 kJ, 314 kcal, 20 g protein, 10 g fat (5 g saturated fat), 35 g carbohydrate (3 g sugars), 7 g fibre, 718 mg sodium

4 large field or portobello mushrooms, about 100 g (3½ oz) each

2 spring onions (scallions)

2 cups (200 g) fresh breadcrumbs

1 cup (100 g) grated parmesan or cheddar

2 tablespoons chopped fresh parsley, thyme or coriander (cilantro)

1 Preheat the oven to 180°C (350°F/Gas 4). Line a baking tray with baking (parchment) paper. Wipe the mushrooms clean with a damp cloth, then remove the stems and coarsely chop them. Finely chop the spring onions.

2 Heat 2 tablespoons olive oil in a large frying pan over medium–high heat. Add the chopped mushroom stems and breadcrumbs and cook, stirring constantly, for 3–4 minutes, or until the crumbs are crunchy.

3 Tip the mixture into a bowl. Add three-quarters of the cheese and all the parsley and spring onions and mix well. Spoon the mixture into each upturned mushroom cup and sprinkle with the remaining cheese.

4 Place the mushrooms on the baking tray and bake for 10 minutes. Serve immediately.

## Variations

• Add some blanched spinach or cooked pumpkin (winter squash) to the stuffing mixture.
• Use chopped fresh thyme, oregano or coriander (cilantro) instead of the parsley.
• Try Japanese breadcrumbs ('panko') instead of fresh breadcrumbs; you'll find these in Asian grocery stores, delicatessens and larger supermarkets.

# Fluffy mashed potatoes

**750 g (1½ lb) mashing potatoes, such as spunta, sebago, pontiac or coliban**

**2 tablespoons butter**

**⅓–½ cup (80–125 ml) milk, approximately**

1  Fill an electric kettle with water and bring to a boil. Pour the water into a large saucepan, add some salt, then cover and return to a boil over high heat.

2  Meanwhile, peel the potatoes and cut them into 2 cm (¾ inch) chunks. Gently place them in the boiling water and cook, uncovered, for 10–12 minutes, or until the potatoes are tender but not falling apart. Drain well, then return the potatoes to the saucepan and mash roughly using a fork or potato masher.

3  While the potatoes are cooking, warm the milk in a separate saucepan over low heat (or in the microwave, uncovered, on high for 1–2 minutes).

4  Chop the butter and add to the potatoes with most of the hot milk. Beat with a wooden spoon until fluffy. Taste and season with salt and freshly ground black pepper. Add the remaining milk if a softer consistency is preferred. Serve immediately.

## Variations

- For a creamier texture and flavour, substitute half the milk with room-temperature cream, sour cream or natural (plain) yogurt.
- Heat 3–4 finely sliced garlic cloves or some finely sliced spring onions with the milk.
- Add chopped fresh herbs, such as parsley or chives.
- Spread the mashed potato in a flat heatproof dish. Rake the surface with a fork and sprinkle with chopped butter and sesame seeds or grated tasty cheese. Cook under a medium–high grill (broiler) or bake in a 230°C (450°F/Gas 8) oven for 5–8 minutes, or until golden on top.

**PREPARATION** 10 minutes

**COOKING** 15 minutes

**SERVES** 4

## Quick tip

To save time, microwave the potatoes on high for 8–10 minutes, or until they are just tender.

## Cook's tip

Don't use a food processor to mash cooked potatoes as they will become sticky and gluggy.

EACH SERVING PROVIDES
892 kJ, 213 kcal, 5 g protein, 9 g fat (6 g saturated fat), 26 g carbohydrate (2 g sugars), 3 g fibre, 87 mg sodium

vegetables

# Spinach & lentil curry

PREPARATION 10 minutes

COOKING 10 minutes

SERVES 4

## Variations

● For a milder and creamier sauce, add natural (plain) yogurt or coconut milk to the curry.
● Replace the lentils with chickpeas or mixed beans.

EACH SERVING PROVIDES
662 kJ, 158 kcal, 7 g protein, 8 g fat
(2 g saturated fat), 15 g carbohydrate
(7 g sugars), 6 g fibre, 965 mg sodium

1 cup (250 ml) Indian-style curry sauce (such as korma or rogan josh), from a jar or can

1 large brown (yellow) onion

420 g (15 oz) can lentils

250 g (8 oz) baby spinach leaves

2 tablespoons chopped fresh coriander (cilantro) leaves

1  Pour the curry sauce and ¾ cup (180 ml) water into a large saucepan and bring to a boil.

2  Meanwhile, peel the onion and cut into wedges. Add the onion to the curry sauce and simmer over medium–low heat for 5 minutes.

3  Drain and rinse the lentils, then drain again. Stir the lentils into the curry with the spinach leaves and simmer for 2–3 minutes, or until the spinach has wilted and the lentils have heated through.

4  Serve garnished with the coriander.

**Serving suggestion**
Serve with steamed basmati or jasmine rice (Thai fragrant rice).

vegetables

# Mini bean casseroles

1 chorizo sausage, about 150 g (5 oz)

1 green or red capsicum (bell pepper)

2 x 420 g (15 oz) cans mixed beans

800 g (16 oz) can chopped tomatoes with herbs

⅓ cup (35 g) grated pecorino or parmesan

1  Preheat the grill (broiler) to high. Dice the chorizo and capsicum. Drain and rinse the beans, then drain again.

2  Place a large saucepan over medium–high heat. Add the chorizo and cook for 2 minutes, stirring occasionally. Reduce the heat to medium, stir in the tomatoes, capsicum and beans and simmer for 6–8 minutes.

3  Divide the mixture among four 1 cup (250 ml) heatproof ramekins and sprinkle with the cheese. Grill (broil) for 2 minutes, or until the cheese has melted. Serve immediately.

PREPARATION 5 minutes

COOKING 15 minutes

SERVES 4

## Variations

● Add chopped black olives, fresh basil, oregano or thyme.
● Sprinkle the casseroles with breadcrumbs.
● Use bacon instead of chorizo.

EACH SERVING PROVIDES
1139 kJ, 272 kcal, 17 g protein, 10 g fat (5 g saturated fat), 27 g carbohydrate (10 g sugars), 10 g fibre, 1028 mg sodium

vegetables

# Glazed vegetables

**PREPARATION** 10 minutes

**COOKING** 15 minutes

**SERVES** 4

## Cook's tip

Instead of being boiled, the vegetables could be steamed for 8–10 minutes, or baked in a preheated 200°C (400°F/Gas 6) oven for 10 minutes, or until they are just tender.

EACH SERVING PROVIDES
531 kJ, 127 kcal, 4 g protein, <1 g fat
(0 g saturated fat), 27 g carbohydrate
(23 g sugars), 6 g fibre, 623 mg sodium

The vegetables can be parboiled the day before. Cool the hot vegetables in a large bowl of iced water, then drain and refrigerate. Simply reheat them in the glaze just before serving.

**2 parsnips, about 150 g (5 oz) each**
**2 carrots, about 150 g (5 oz) each**
**2 turnips, about 150 g (5 oz) each**
**¼ cup (80 g) good-quality lime and ginger marmalade**
**¼ cup (60 ml) Japanese soy sauce**

1 Fill an electric kettle with water and bring to a boil. Pour the water into a saucepan, add some salt and return to a boil. Meanwhile, peel the vegetables and cut into batons about 5 cm (2 inches) long and 2 cm (¾ inch) thick.

2 Add the vegetables to the pot and gently boil for 7–8 minutes, or until slightly tender but not soft. Drain.

3 Place the marmalade and soy sauce in a saucepan or frying pan large enough to hold all the vegetables. Stir in 1 tablespoon water and 1 tablespoon extra virgin olive oil and bring to a boil over medium heat, stirring occasionally.

4 Add the vegetables and toss gently for a few minutes, or until the vegetables are coated in the mixture and a glaze forms on them. Season with salt and freshly ground black pepper and serve immediately.

## Variations
- Substitute or add other vegetables, such as potato, sweet potato, Jerusalem artichokes or jicama.
- Add fresh thyme or rosemary leaves.
- Instead of marmalade, use jam, maple syrup or sugar.
- For a richer flavour, use butter instead of olive oil in step 3.

# Vegetable risoni

250 g (8 oz) cherry tomatoes

400 g (14 oz) broccoli

350 g (12 oz) thin asparagus spears

375 g (13 oz) risoni (rice-shaped pasta) or other pasta

250 g (8 oz) jar goat's cheese, marinated in herbs and oil

PREPARATION 10 minutes

COOKING 15 minutes

SERVES 4

1  Preheat the oven to 220°C (425°F/Gas7). Line a baking tray with baking (parchment) paper. Cut the tomatoes in half, place on the baking tray and season with salt and freshly ground black pepper. Bake for 10–15 minutes, or until the tomatoes are hot and slightly shrivelled.

2  Meanwhile, fill an electric kettle with water and bring to a boil. Cut the broccoli into florets; trim the asparagus and cut each spear into three or four lengths.

3  Pour the boiling water into a large saucepan, then cover and return to a boil over high heat. Season the water with a good pinch of salt and add the risoni. Cover and return to a boil, then cook, uncovered, for 6 minutes, or according to the packet instructions, until al dente. About 2 minutes before the risoni is cooked, add the broccoli and asparagus to the water and cook for 2 minutes, or until just tender.

4  Drain the risoni and vegetables and return to the pan. Crumble the goat's cheese over the top, drizzle with some of the cheese marinating oil and toss to combine. Serve immediately, topped with the tomatoes.

## Shortcut ingredients

Instead of baking the cherry tomatoes, you could just toss some chopped semi-dried (sun-blushed) tomatoes through the pasta.

EACH SERVING PROVIDES
2454 kJ, 586 kcal, 31 g protein, 20 g fat (13 g saturated fat), 69 g carbohydrate (4 g sugars), 9 g fibre, 355 mg sodium

## Variations

- Instead of goat's cheese, use fetta, parmesan or blue cheese.
- Use other vegetables, such as broad (fava) beans, peas, or sliced yellow or green beans.
- Add canned lentils or chickpeas, fresh chopped herbs or lemon juice.
- Toss some sour cream or yogurt through the pasta.

# Brussels sprouts, pancetta & almonds

**PREPARATION** 5 minutes

**COOKING** 10 minutes

**SERVES** 4

## Shopping tip

If fresh brussels sprouts are not in season or are quite expensive, buy a packet of frozen brussels sprouts instead.

EACH SERVING PROVIDES
522 kJ, 124 kcal, 10 g protein, 7 g fat
(1 g saturated fat), 4 g carbohydrate
(4 g sugars), 6 g fibre, 296 mg sodium

For the very best flavour, buy brussels sprouts with firm, heavy, compact heads and smooth, bright-green leaves. Choose sprouts of a similar size, so they'll all cook at the same time.

**500 g (1 lb) brussels sprouts**
**¼ cup (30 g) slivered almonds**
**1 red capsicum (bell pepper)**
**75 g (2½ oz) pancetta**
**1 clove garlic**

1   Fill an electric kettle with water and bring to a boil. Pour the water into a large saucepan and return to a boil. Meanwhile, trim the brussels sprouts, leaving a small amount of stalk attached so they don't fall apart during cooking. Leave the sprouts whole if they are small; otherwise cut them in half lengthwise. Add them to the boiling water and cook for 3 minutes, then carefully empty them into a colander and leave to drain.

2   Meanwhile, put the almonds in a large, dry frying pan and toast over medium heat for 2–3 minutes, or until golden, stirring occasionally to stop them burning. Tip the almonds into a bowl.

3   Thinly slice the capsicum and pancetta; crush the garlic. Increase the heat to medium–high and add 1 tablespoon olive oil to the frying pan. Once the oil is hot, add the capsicum, pancetta and garlic and cook, stirring occasionally, for 5–6 minutes, or until the capsicum has softened and the pancetta is crisp.

4   Add the brussels sprouts and toss to combine. Season with salt and freshly ground black pepper. Serve immediately, sprinkled with almonds.

## Variations
- Add chopped fresh thyme or sage leaves, or grated fresh ginger.
- Add or substitute chopped broccoli or sliced zucchini (courgette).
- Instead of almonds use pine nuts, or sesame seeds and sesame oil.

# Roast vegetables

**PREPARATION** 10 minutes

**COOKING** 15 minutes

**SERVES** 4

## Cook's tip

If you have any roast vegetables left over, toss them through salads, frittatas and dishes like bubble 'n' squeak.

EACH SERVING PROVIDES
429 kJ, 102 kcal, 4 g protein, <1 g fat (0 g saturated fat), 21 g carbohydrate (15 g sugars), 7 g fibre, 86 mg sodium

2 beetroot (beets), about 150 g (5 oz) each, with stems

300 g (10 oz) orange sweet potatoes

2 small or baby fennel bulbs, about 200 g (7 oz) each

1 tablespoon balsamic vinegar

8 fresh rosemary sprigs

1  Preheat the oven to 230°C (450°F/Gas 8). Line a baking tray with baking (parchment) paper.

2  Wash and trim the beetroot, then cut into wedges 1 cm (½ inch) thick, leaving about 5 cm (2 inches) of stem still attached. Peel the sweet potato and cut into batons about 5 cm (2 inches) long and 2 cm (¾ inch) thick. Cut the fennel into quarters.

3  Place the vegetables on the baking tray. Drizzle with the vinegar and 1 tablespoon olive oil, sprinkle with salt and freshly ground black pepper and toss until the vegetables are well coated.

4  Strip the rosemary leaves off their stems and scatter over the vegetables. Bake for 15 minutes, turning once. Serve immediately.

## Variations
- Use other vegetables, such as small new potatoes, turnips, carrots, Jerusalem artichokes and onion wedges.
- Try different fresh herbs, such as thyme or lemon thyme.

# Thai pumpkin & eggplant curry

500 g (1 lb) pumpkin (winter squash)

300 g (10 oz) Lebanese or Thai eggplants (aubergines)

4 tablespoons Thai red curry paste, or to taste

270 ml (9½ fl oz) can light coconut cream

4 tablespoons chopped coriander (cilantro) leaves

1  Peel the pumpkin and cut into 2.5 cm (1 inch) dice. Trim and slice the eggplants.

2  Heat 1 tablespoon peanut oil or corn oil in a large saucepan over medium heat. Add the curry paste and fry gently for 2 minutes, or until the paste begins to release its fragrant aromas, stirring occasionally.

3  Stir in the coconut cream and ½ cup (125 ml) water and bring to a boil. Add the pumpkin and eggplants, reduce the heat and simmer for 10–12 minutes, or until the pumpkin is tender.

4  Serve in small bowls, garnished with the coriander.

### Serving suggestion
Serve with jasmine rice (Thai fragrant rice) or cooked rice noodles.

## Variations
- Add other vegetables such as peas, or chopped onion, potato, carrot and green beans.
- For extra protein, add canned chickpeas or lentils, or diced tofu, beef, chicken or firm fish fillets.
- Instead of red curry paste, try a green or massaman curry paste and add 2–3 teaspoons sugar to reduce the curry 'heat'.
- Instead of coriander, use Thai basil leaves and/or thinly sliced makrut (kaffir lime) leaves. (If using lime leaves, first remove the stems by folding the leaf in half and pulling the spine downwards.)

PREPARATION 10 minutes

COOKING 15 minutes

SERVES 4

## Shopping tip
The long, thin Lebanese eggplant and small, round Thai eggplant are available (when in season) from good greengrocers and Asian grocery stores.

## Cook's tip
There is no need to salt Lebanese or Thai eggplant.

EACH SERVING PROVIDES
747 kJ, 178 kcal, 5 g protein, 12 g fat (9 g saturated fat), 13 g carbohydrate (9 g sugars), 3 g fibre, 38 mg sodium

vegetables

# Okra with onion & tomato

## Shortcut ingredients

Using frozen okra will reduce the cooking time to 8–10 minutes.

EACH SERVING PROVIDES
329 kJ, 78 kcal, 4 g protein, <1 g fat
(0 g saturated fat), 15 g carbohydrate
(11 g sugars), 5 g fibre, 259 mg sodium

175 g (6 oz) fresh okra

1 large brown (yellow) onion

1 green capsicum (bell pepper)

800 g (16 oz) can chopped tomatoes with herbs

2 tablespoons worcestershire sauce

1  Wash and trim the okra and cut each into three or four pieces. Peel the onion and cut into wedges. Chop the capsicum into bite-sized pieces.

2  Place the tomatoes in a large saucepan. Add the worcestershire sauce, okra, onion and capsicum, and season to taste with salt and freshly ground black pepper. Stir well and simmer over medium heat for 12–15 minutes, or until the okra is tender.

3  Serve immediately, or allow to cool, then cover and refrigerate until required. Reheat in a saucepan or microwave to serve.

# Potatoes with corn & capsicum

8 small new potatoes, about 60 g (2 oz) each

2 corn cobs

2 rindless bacon slices (bacon strips)

1 red capsicum (bell pepper)

½ cup (40 g) fetta, marinated in herbs and oil

PREPARATION 5 minutes

COOKING 15 minutes

SERVES 4

1 Fill an electric kettle with water and bring to a boil. Meanwhile, wash the potatoes and cut them in half lengthwise. Place in a large saucepan and pour enough boiling water over to cover well. Bring to a boil over high heat and cook, uncovered, for 12–15 minutes, or until tender. Drain.

2 Meanwhile, stand each corn cob upright on a chopping board, then cut down the sides with a sharp knife to remove the kernels. Place the kernels in a large frying pan with ½ cup (125 ml) water and cook over medium–high heat for 3–4 minutes, or until softened. Drain.

3 Place the frying pan back over high heat. Finely chop the bacon and capsicum and cook for 4–5 minutes, stirring occasionally. Stir in the corn.

4 Place the potatoes on serving plates and top with the corn mixture. Crumble the fetta over the top, drizzle with some of the fetta marinating oil and serve.

## Variations

- For a creamier topping, mix some canned creamed corn through the corn mixture.
- Add sliced spring onions (scallions), blanched spinach leaves or chopped fresh parsley.
- Top with grated tasty cheddar and sour cream instead of fetta.

EACH SERVING PROVIDES
962 kJ, 230 kcal, 13 g protein, 6 g fat
(3 g saturated fat), 30 g carbohydrate
(3 g sugars), 6 g fibre, 376 mg sodium

vegetables

# Sweet potato couscous

This versatile salad is great at barbecues, and pairs particularly well with chargrilled lamb cutlets or lamb fillets.

**500 g (1 lb) orange sweet potatoes**
**¾ cup (110 g) seed and nut mix (available from supermarkets)**
**2 cups (270 g) instant couscous**
**1 large lemon**
**1½ tablespoons of your favourite spice mix**

1  Preheat the oven to 220°C (425°F/Gas 7). Line two baking trays with baking (parchment) paper.

2  Peel the sweet potato, cut into 2 cm (¾ inch) squares and place on one of the baking trays. Drizzle with 1 tablespoon olive oil, toss until evenly coated, then season with salt and freshly ground black pepper. Scatter the seed mix on the other baking tray. Bake the sweet potato for 5 minutes, then add the seed mix to the oven and bake with the sweet potato for a further 5 minutes.

3  Meanwhile, bring 2 cups (500 ml) water to a boil in an electric kettle. Put the couscous in a large heatproof bowl and pour the boiling water over. Stir in 2 tablespoons olive oil, then cover and leave to soak for 5 minutes, or until the liquid has been absorbed.

4  Zest and juice the lemon; finely chop the zest. Fluff the couscous with a fork, breaking up any lumps. Add 1 teaspoon lemon zest, 3 tablespoons lemon juice, the spice mix and salt and freshly ground black pepper to taste, mixing well. Gently fold the sweet potato and seed mix through. Serve warm, or refrigerate and serve cold.

## Variations
- For a richer flavour, soak the couscous in hot stock or orange juice instead of water; replace the olive oil with melted butter.
- Stir in chopped fresh coriander (cilantro), mint or parsley.
- Add canned chickpeas, currants and chopped olives or dates.

**PREPARATION** 10 minutes
**COOKING** 10 minutes
**SERVES** 4

## Cook's tip
For extra flavour, heat the spices in a frying pan over medium heat for 2–3 minutes, or until fragrant, stirring so they don't burn. The seeds and nuts can also be toasted in the frying pan for 2–3 minutes — shake the pan occasionally so they don't burn.

EACH SERVING PROVIDES
1825 kJ, 436 kcal, 14 g protein, 8 g fat (1 g saturated fat), 75 g carbohydrate (10 g sugars), 5 g fibre, 24 mg sodium

vegetables

# Creamy herbed potatoes

PREPARATION 15 minutes

COOKING 15 minutes

SERVES 4

## Shopping tip

For this recipe, look for potatoes that are labelled 'waxy', 'new' or 'boiling' potatoes. These have a high moisture content and hold their shape during cooking.

EACH SERVING PROVIDES
665 kJ, 158 kcal, 7 g protein, 2 g fat
(1 g saturated fat), 27 g carbohydrate
(3 g sugars), 4 g fibre, 34 mg sodium

**750 g (1½ lb) potatoes**

**2 cloves garlic**

**3 tablespoons chopped fresh parsley**

**3 tablespoons chopped fresh mint**

**¾ cup (185 g) natural (plain) yogurt**

1  Fill an electric kettle with water and bring to a boil. Pour the water into a saucepan, add some salt and return to a boil.

2  Meanwhile, wash the potatoes and cut into 2.5 cm (1 inch) dice, leaving the skin on if preferred. Gently lower them into the boiling water and cook for 10–12 minutes, or until tender.

3  While the potatoes are cooking, crush the garlic. Combine in a bowl with the yogurt, stir in the herbs and season to taste with salt and freshly ground black pepper.

4  Gently mix the potatoes through the yogurt dressing. Serve warm, or refrigerate and serve cold.

## Variations

• Flavour the dressing with wholegrain mustard or wasabi; or substitute the yogurt with sour cream or soft cream cheese.
• For a more substantial dish, add cooked or canned tuna or salmon, or barbecued chicken.
• Substitute half the potatoes with orange sweet potato.
• Add or substitute blanched spinach and chopped red capsicum (bell pepper), spring onions (scallions) or coriander (cilantro).
• Turn the dish into a gratin: spread the cooked potato mixture in a wide, shallow dish. Sprinkle with sesame seeds, breadcrumbs or grated cheese and brown under a medium–high grill (broiler) before serving.

# Satay vegetables

300 g (10 oz) broccoli

300 g (10 oz) cauliflower

1 red capsicum (bell pepper)

1 cup (250 ml) satay sauce

4 tablespoons chopped fresh coriander (cilantro) leaves

1 Cut the broccoli and cauliflower into florets; cut the capsicum into 2.5 cm (1 inch) squares.

2 Heat 1 tablespoon peanut or rice bran oil in a large wok or frying pan over medium–high heat. Add the broccoli, cauliflower and capsicum and stir-fry for 2–3 minutes, or until just tender but still crisp.

3 Pour the satay sauce over the vegetables and toss to combine. Cook for 1–2 minutes, or until heated through. Serve immediately, sprinkled with the coriander.

### Serving suggestion

Serve with jasmine rice (Thai fragrant rice), soba or rice noodles. Fried Asian shallots make a delicious crunchy garnish; you'll find these in Asian grocery stores.

## Variations

- Add some cubed tofu.
- For a milder sauce, add yogurt, coconut cream or coconut milk.

PREPARATION 5 minutes

COOKING 5 minutes

SERVES 4

## Shortcut ingredient

To save time, use pre-packaged stir-fry vegetables.

## Cook's tip

You can use satay sauce from a jar or can, but it is also very quick and easy to make your own — see our recipe in Basics.

EACH SERVING PROVIDES
1110 kJ, 265 kcal, 9 g protein, 16 g fat (5 g saturated fat), 20 g carbohydrate (13 g sugars), 6 g fibre, 470 mg sodium

vegetables

# Vegetable tarts

PREPARATION 10 minutes

COOKING 5 minutes

SERVES 4

## Shortcut ingredient

Frozen mixed vegetables can also be used.

## Cook's tip

The won ton wrappers can be baked ahead and stored in an airtight container.

EACH SERVING PROVIDES
1269 kJ, 303 kcal, 14 g protein, 9 g fat
(2 g saturated fat), 40 g carbohydrate
(6 g sugars), 4 g fibre, 698 mg sodium

Won ton wrappers make a super-speedy and super-simple pastry case for these tasty and endlessly variable little tarts.

**12 won ton wrappers**

**1 small red capsicum (bell pepper)**

**3 x 125 g (4 oz) cans creamed corn**

**2 x 95 g (3½ oz) cans flavoured tuna (such as lemon, or tomato and onion)**

**1 tablespoon dried mixed herbs**

1  Preheat the oven to 230°C (450°F/Gas 8). Lightly spray the won ton wrappers on each side with canola or rice bran oil spray. Gently press the wrappers into a 12-hole standard muffin tin and bake for 4–5 minutes, or until crisp and golden.

2  Meanwhile, dice the capsicum, then place in a large saucepan over medium heat. Stir in the creamed corn, tuna and herbs and cook for 5 minutes, or until warmed through.

3  Spoon the mixture into the wrappers and serve immediately.

## Variations

● Add chopped marinated semi-dried tomatoes, asparagus, celery, blanched spinach, chives or spring onions (scallions) to the filling.
● Instead of tuna, try barbecued chicken or chopped ham.
● Spoon the filling into ready-made pastry cases, or wrap them in puff or filo pastry and bake until lightly browned.
● Use sliced bread for the pastry cases. Remove the crusts and flatten each slice with a rolling pin, then lightly spray both sides with oil and push into the muffin tin. Bake in a 190°C (375°F/Gas 5) oven until lightly browned and crisp.

# Vegetable patties

PREPARATION 10 minutes

COOKING about 10 minutes

SERVES 4 (makes 8)

## Cook's tip

The pattie mixture is quite soft and needs to be handled carefully; for a firmer texture, add 1 small lightly beaten egg. The patties can be shaped ahead of time and refrigerated until required.

EACH SERVING (2 PATTIES) PROVIDES
1624 kJ, 388 kcal, 17 g protein, 19 g fat
(4 g saturated fat), 39 g carbohydrate
(4 g sugars), 10 g fibre, 838 mg sodium

2 x 420 g (15 oz) cans mixed beans

1½ cups (120 g) fresh breadcrumbs

1 teaspoon ground cumin

2 tablespoons chopped fresh coriander (cilantro) leaves, mint or parsley

1 cup (250 g) tzatziki (see Basics) or natural (plain) yogurt

1 Drain and rinse the beans, then drain again. Place in a food processor with the breadcrumbs, cumin and coriander. Season with salt and freshly ground black pepper and process until the mixture is roughly chopped but will hold together. Using clean hands, gently knead the mixture so it comes together, then shape the mixture into eight patties.

2 Heat a large frying pan over medium heat, then add enough vegetable oil to cover the base. Once the oil is hot, cook the patties, in two batches if necessary, for 2–3 minutes on each side, or until golden on both sides.

3 Serve immediately, with the tzatziki or yogurt.

## Variations

● Use other canned beans or legumes, such as soybeans, chickpeas or cannellini beans.
● Mix in other ingredients, such as grated zucchini (courgette) or carrot, chopped spring onions (scallions) and fresh parsley or mint.

desserts

# Classic ways with ice cream

Forget gourmet ice creams. If you keep a tub of plain vanilla ice cream in the freezer, you can conjure up an infinitely yummy range of desserts in no time at all.

## A sprinkling of fun

Add any of the following to a bowl of vanilla ice cream, or make an ice cream sundae by layering a combination of ingredients in a tall, clear glass.

### Go nuts

Use any type of lightly toasted nut, such as walnuts, pecans, flaked or slivered almonds, pistachios or peanuts. To toast raw nuts, spread them on a baking tray and bake in a preheated 180°C (350°F/Gas 4) oven for a few minutes. Keep an eye on them as they can burn quickly; cool before using. Shredded coconut can be toasted in a dry frying pan over medium heat for about 2 minutes.

### Sweet treats

Try chopped chocolate or other candy bars, marshmallows, cake-decorating sprinkles, chocolate chips or candy-coated chocolate buttons — whatever takes your fancy!

### Crazy about crumbs

Sprinkle crushed or chopped biscuits (cookies) over the ice cream, or serve a special variety (like a gourmet shortbread, chewy coconut macaroon or crunchy biscotti) on the side.

### Lusciously fruity

Any berries, fresh or frozen, are divine with ice cream — use fresh seasonal fruits, or canned fruit for convenience. Or soak some dried fruit in a little orange juice or alcohol until plump, then spoon the whole lot over the ice cream.

## A touch of class

Here are some surprisingly simple ways to dress up ice cream. These are desserts you could easily dish up if you're entertaining.

### It's a wrap

Sandwich a scoop of ice cream between two chocolate biscuits (cookies) and gently squeeze together. Make as many as you need, then serve straight away, or wrap each one tightly in plastic and freeze to serve later.

### Rhubarb surprise

Chop some rhubarb and place in a saucepan with sugar to taste. (Add a cinnamon stick or pinch of ground cinnamon if desired.) Cover and simmer for 5–10 minutes, or until the rhubarb is soft and pulpy. Serve with vanilla ice cream, with a gourmet shortbread on the side.

### Takes the cake

Cut a ready-made sponge cake or chocolate cake in half horizontally. Top the base with small scoops of ice cream, then replace the top. Drizzle with chocolate or another sauce, cut into wedges and serve immediately.

### Italian affogato

Scoop some vanilla ice cream into small heatproof glasses, then drizzle with a little of your favourite liqueur (Frangelico is especially good). Pour strong, freshly brewed espresso coffee over the top and serve immediately.

# A dreamy drizzle

Ice cream loves a lavish slurp of any of the sauces below. For an instant fuss-free, fruity sauce, nothing beats a scoop of fresh passionfruit!

## Chocolate fudge sauce

**MAKES** about 1 cup (250 ml)

½ cup (125 ml) pouring (light) cream
1 tablespoon butter
¼ cup (45 g) soft brown sugar
100 g (3½ oz) good-quality dark chocolate
1 teaspoon vanilla extract

Combine the cream, butter and sugar in a small saucepan. Stir over medium–low heat until the butter has melted and the sugar has dissolved. Bring to a boil, then remove from the heat. Break up the chocolate, add to the pan and stand for 5 minutes, or until it has softened. Stir until smooth, then stir in the vanilla. Serve warm, or at room temperature.

## Strawberry sauce

**MAKES** about ¾ cup (180 ml)

250 g (8 oz) strawberries
1 tablespoon icing (confectioners') sugar
2 teaspoons lemon juice

Wash the strawberries, remove the hulls and pat the fruit dry with paper towels. Place in a food processor with the remaining ingredients and process until smooth. Pour the mixture into a fine sieve over a jug, then press with the back of a spoon to remove the seeds and make a smooth sauce. Serve at room temperature, or slightly chilled.

**VARIATION** Use raspberries instead of strawberries. Add a dash of your favourite liqueur, such as Grand Marnier.

## Nutty caramel sauce

**MAKES** about ¾ cup (180 ml)

½ cup (110 g) caster (superfine) sugar
½ cup (125 ml) pouring (light) cream
¼ cup (35 g) toasted slivered almonds

Combine the sugar and ¼ cup (60 ml) water in a small saucepan. Stir over low heat without boiling until the sugar has dissolved, then increase the heat to medium and bring to a boil. Cook for 7 minutes, or until the syrup turns deep golden brown. Remove from the heat and carefully add the cream (it may spit as it hits the hot caramel). The toffee will turn lumpy, so return to low heat and stir for 2 minutes, or until the toffee melts and the sauce is smooth. Stir in the almonds. Serve warm, or at room temperature.

**VARIATION** Use chopped toasted pecans, walnuts or hazelnuts.

## Butterscotch sauce

**MAKES** about 1¼ cups (310 ml)

2½ tablespoons butter
½ cup (100 g) soft brown sugar
½ cup (125 ml) pouring (light) cream
1 teaspoon vanilla extract

Chop the butter and place in a saucepan with the sugar, cream and vanilla. Stir over medium heat for 3 minutes, or until smooth. Serve warm, or at room temperature.

## Chocolate liqueur sauce

**MAKES** about 1½ cups (375 ml)

½ cup (125 ml) pouring (light) cream
150 g (5 oz) good-quality dark chocolate
1 tablespoon liqueur, such as Grand Marnier,
  Tia Maria or rum

Bring the cream to a boil in a small saucepan over medium heat. Remove from the heat. Break up the chocolate, add to the pan and stand for 5 minutes, or until the chocolate has softened. Stir until smooth, then stir in the liqueur. Serve warm, or at room temperature.

# Passionfruit fool

**200 ml (7 fl oz) pouring (light) cream**
**2 tablespoons icing (confectioners') sugar**
**1 teaspoon vanilla extract**
**⅔ cup (150 ml) passionfruit pulp**
**8 almond bread or biscotti, to serve**

1 Using electric beaters, whip the cream, icing sugar and vanilla in a bowl until soft peaks form.

2 Using a large metal spoon or rubber spatula, gently fold most of the passionfruit pulp into the cream, reserving a little for decorating — don't stir too vigorously or you will spoil the lovely texture of the cream.

3 Spoon the mixture into four ⅔ cup (150 ml) serving glasses. Drizzle the remaining passionfruit pulp over the top. Serve with the almond bread or biscotti on the side.

PREPARATION 10 minutes

COOKING none

SERVES 4

## Cook's tip
This dessert can be served straight away, or made up to 2 hours ahead and chilled until serving time.

EACH SERVING PROVIDES
1404 kJ, 335 kcal, 4 g protein, 25 g fat (15 g saturated fat), 26 g carbohydrate (22 g sugars), 5 g fibre, 18 mg sodium

# Cherry crepes

PREPARATION 10 minutes

COOKING 5 minutes

SERVES 4

## Cook's tip

If time permits, make your own crepes. See our recipe in Basics.

## Shortcut ingredient

Using frozen, bottled or canned cherries for this recipe saves time as you won't need to pit them.

EACH SERVING PROVIDES
2031 kJ, 485 kcal, 9 g protein, 22 g fat
(13 g saturated fat), 56 g carbohydrate
(32 g sugars), 4 g fibre, 66 mg sodium

**8 frozen crepes (from the freezer cabinet of supermarkets)**
**750 g (1½ lb) cherries**
**2 tablespoons kirsch or cherry liqueur**
**2 tablespoons caster (superfine) sugar**
**½ cup (125 ml) thick (double) cream**

1  Lay the crepes out on a bench to thaw.

2  Place the cherries in a large frying pan with the kirsch, sugar and 1 tablespoon water. Cook over medium heat for 5 minutes, or until the cherries have softened and released some juice, stirring occasionally to dissolve the sugar.

3  Meanwhile, warm the crepes according to the packet instructions.

4  Place two crepes on each serving plate. Top with the cherries, then fold or roll to enclose. Drizzle with the syrup from the pan, top with a dollop of cream and serve.

## Variation

You can omit the kirsch, and increase the water quantity in step 2 to 2 tablespoons.

# Pears with walnuts & sultanas

PREPARATION 10 minutes

COOKING 10 minutes

SERVES 4

## Quick tip

The cooking time is greatly reduced in this recipe by using a microwave. In a conventional oven, the pears will take a good 30–40 minutes to cook at 190°C (375°F/Gas 5).

EACH SERVING PROVIDES
598 kJ, 143 kcal, 1 g protein, 3 g fat
(<1 g saturated fat), 28 g carbohydrate
(24 g sugars), 3 g fibre, 6 mg sodium

**4 small ripe pears**

**¼ cup (30 g) sultanas (golden raisins)**

**2 tablespoons walnut pieces**

**½ teaspoon ground cinnamon**

**1 tablespoon honey**

1  Peel the pears, cut them in half lengthwise and scoop out the cores. Place the pear halves in a shallow, round microwave-safe dish, with the wide ends of the pears around the edge of the dish.

2  Combine the sultanas, walnuts and cinnamon in a bowl, then sprinkle evenly over the pears. Mix the honey with 2 teaspoons water and drizzle over the pears.

3  Cover and microwave on medium–high for 8–12 minutes, or until the pears are tender.

4  Serve drizzled with the juices from the bottom of the dish.

**Serving suggestion**
Serve with ice cream or yogurt.

## Variation

- Use toasted flaked almonds instead of walnuts.
- If pears are not available, granny smith apples (or other dessert or cooking apples), can also be cooked in this way.

# Apricot gratin

PREPARATION 10 minutes

COOKING 5 minutes

SERVES 4

## Shopping tip

Orange blossom water (or orange flower water) is mainly sold in specialty food shops.

EACH SERVING PROVIDES
824 kJ, 197 kcal, 3 g protein, 15 g fat (10 g saturated fat), 13 g carbohydrate (12 g sugars), 2 g fibre, 17 mg sodium

800 g (16 oz) can apricot halves (you can also use canned peach halves)

2 teaspoons orange blossom water (optional)

125 g (4 oz) mascarpone, creamy yogurt or crème fraîche

1 tablespoon soft brown sugar

2 tablespoons unsalted, shelled pistachios

1 Preheat the grill (broiler) to high. Drain the apricots and arrange them in a heatproof dish, cut side up.

2 Mix the orange blossom water, if using, through the mascarpone. Dollop a little mascarpone into each apricot half, then sprinkle with the sugar. Grill (broil) for 5 minutes, or until the sugar has melted and is bubbling on top.

3 Chop the pistachios, sprinkle over the apricots and serve.

# Caramelised apples on raisin toast

3 large granny smith, dessert or cooking apples,
  about 350 g (12 oz) in total
30 g (1 oz) butter
⅓ cup (80 ml) maple syrup
4 thick slices raisin bread
4 scoops vanilla ice cream

PREPARATION 10 minutes

COOKING 10 minutes

SERVES 4

## Variation

Instead of raisin bread, serve
the apples on toasted brioche,
panettone or any type of fruit
bread you like.

EACH SERVING PROVIDES
1347 kJ, 322 kcal, 4 g protein, 10 g fat
(6 g saturated fat), 56 g carbohydrate
(42 g sugars), 4 g fibre, 144 mg sodium

1  Peel, quarter and core the apples, then cut each quarter into three
wedges. Melt the butter in a large non-stick frying pan over medium
heat. Add the apples, spreading them out in a single layer, or as much
as possible. Sprinkle 2 tablespoons water over.

2  Cook the apples, turning occasionally, for 8 minutes, or until tender.
Drizzle with the maple syrup and cook for a further 2 minutes, turning
the apples to coat in the buttery syrup.

3  Toast the bread, cut each slice diagonally in half if you wish, then
place on serving plates. Spoon the apples over and drizzle with any
remaining syrup. Top with a scoop of ice cream and serve immediately.

# Peach trifle

800 g (28 oz) can sliced peaches in natural juice
500 g (1 lb) plain sponge cake (see Basics)
2 cups (500 ml) custard (see Basics)
2 tablespoons flaked almonds
300 ml (10 fl oz) pouring (light) cream

1  Drain the peaches and reserve ¼ cup (60 ml) of the juice. Cut the sponge cake into 2 cm (¾ inch) pieces.

2  Arrange half the cake pieces in a 1.75 litre (7 cup) glass serving dish and sprinkle with half the reserved peach juice. Top with half the peaches, then pour half the custard over, spreading it out with the back of a spoon. Repeat with the remaining cake, reserved juice, peaches and custard to make another layer.

3  Place the almonds in a dry frying pan and cook over medium heat for 2 minutes, or until lightly toasted, stirring often. Transfer to a plate to cool.

4  Using electric beaters, whip the cream to soft peaks in a bowl. Dollop the cream over the top of the trifle. Sprinkle with the toasted almonds and serve.

## Variations

- Instead of peaches, use different types of canned fruit, such as apricots or pears.
- Use a jam-filled Swiss roll (jelly roll) instead of plain sponge cake.

PREPARATION 10 minutes

COOKING 5 minutes

SERVES 6–8

## Cook's tip

If time allows, assemble the trifle without the cream and almonds, then cover and refrigerate for up to 6 hours for the sponge cake to soften and for the flavours to develop. Top with the cream and almonds just before serving.

EACH SERVING PROVIDES
728 kJ, 174 kcal, 3 g protein, 8 g fat (5 g saturated fat), 23 g carbohydrate (17 g sugars), 1 g fibre, 79 mg sodium

desserts

# Quick apple crumble

PREPARATION 10 minutes

COOKING 5 minutes

SERVES 4

## Shortcut ingredients

For an even quicker crumble, use canned fruit such as pears, peaches or apricots.

EACH SERVING PROVIDES
1305 kJ, 312 kcal, 3 g protein, 12 g fat
(7 g saturated fat), 49 g carbohydrate
(35 g sugars), 6 g fibre, 159 mg sodium

**1 kg (2 lb) granny smith, dessert or cooking apples**
**50 g (1¾ oz) butter**
**¼ cup (35 g) plain (all-purpose) flour**
**2 tablespoons soft brown sugar**
**½ cup (65 g) toasted muesli (one with nuts and coconut)**

1  Peel, core and roughly chop the apples. Place in a saucepan with ¼ cup (60 ml) water. Cover and bring to a boil over medium heat, then reduce the heat to low and cook, covered, for 5–8 minutes, or until soft.

2  Meanwhile, melt the butter in a large deep frying pan over medium heat. Add the flour and stir for 1 minute. Add the sugar and stir for a further minute, then add the muesli. Cook, stirring, for 3 minutes, reducing the heat slightly if necessary, until the mixture is golden brown and nicely toasted, breaking up any clumps with a wooden spoon.

3  Spoon the apples into bowls, top with the crumble mixture and serve.

### Serving suggestion
Custard, cream or ice cream are all delicious with apple crumble!

# Honey-roasted figs

PREPARATION 10 minutes

COOKING 15 minutes

SERVES 4

## Variation

● Bake the figs just with the honey, and serve topped with crème fraîche or vanilla yogurt.
● Replace the ricotta with creamy blue cheese.

EACH SERVING PROVIDES
820 kJ, 196 kcal, 5 g protein, 8 g fat
(2 g saturated fat), 26 g carbohydrate
(26 g sugars), 3 g fibre, 56 mg sodium

¼ **cup (30 g) walnut pieces**

**8 regular-sized ripe figs, or 12 small ripe figs**

**100 g (3½ oz) ricotta**

**3 tablespoons honey**

1  Preheat the oven to 200°C (400°F/Gas 6). Spread the walnuts on a baking tray and roast for 4 minutes, or until just fragrant. Transfer to a plate or board to cool.

2  Meanwhile, use a sharp knife to cut a cross into the top of each fig, without cutting all the way through. Open the figs out slightly, into quarters.

3  Spoon the ricotta into the figs. Stand them upright in a small baking dish, so the ricotta won't fall out. Drizzle with 2 tablespoons of the honey and bake for 10 minutes, or until softened. Meanwhile, finely chop the walnuts.

4  Arrange the figs on serving plates. Drizzle with the remaining honey, sprinkle with the walnuts and serve.

desserts

# Saucy chocolate puddings

½ cup (75 g) self-raising flour

⅓ cup (40 g) unsweetened cocoa powder, plus extra for dusting

½ cup (95 g) soft brown sugar

¼ cup (60 ml) milk

1 egg

PREPARATION 10 minutes

COOKING 15 minutes

SERVES 4

## Cook's tip

Serve the puddings hot, before the sauce that forms at the bottom of each ramekin is absorbed back into the pudding.

EACH SERVING PROVIDES
875 kJ, 209 kcal, 6 g protein, 3 g fat (2 g saturated fat), 39 g carbohydrate (24 g sugars), 1 g fibre, 184 mg sodium

1 Preheat the oven to 190°C (375°F/Gas 5). Lightly grease four 1¼ cup (310 ml) ovenproof ramekins. Sift the flour, half the cocoa powder and half the sugar into a bowl and make a well in the centre.

2 Bring 1½ cups (375 ml) water to a boil in an electric kettle. Whisk the milk and egg in a jug, then gently fold the mixture through the dry ingredients, using a rubber spatula. Spoon the batter into the ramekins.

3 Sift the remaining cocoa powder and sugar together, then sprinkle evenly over the batter in each ramekin. Set the ramekins on a baking tray and slowly pour ⅓ cup (80 ml) boiling water into each ramekin.

4 Bake for 15 minutes, or until the puddings feel firm on top. Dust with extra cocoa powder and serve immediately.

## Serving suggestion
Serve with thick (heavy/double) cream or vanilla ice cream.

# Mixed berry mess

**200 g (7 oz) fresh or frozen mixed berries**
**200 ml (7 fl oz) pouring (light) cream**
**1 teaspoon vanilla extract**
**dark chocolate, for grating**
**50 g (1¾ oz) ready-made meringues**

1 If using frozen berries, spread them on a plate in a single layer and stand at room temperature while you prepare the other ingredients — they only need to partially thaw.

2 Using electric beaters, whip the cream and vanilla in a bowl until soft peaks form. Grate enough chocolate to decorate each dessert (or use a vegetable peeler to shave thin shards from the side of the block).

3 Break the meringues up into small chunks (it doesn't matter if they crumble), dropping them into the cream. Add the berries.

4 Gently fold the berries and meringues into the cream. Spoon into serving dishes, sprinkle with the chocolate and serve.

PREPARATION 10 minutes

COOKING none

SERVES 4

## Cook's tip

This dessert is best served within 30 minutes of assembling. The cream can be whipped up to 2 hours in advance, and kept, tightly covered, in the fridge.

EACH SERVING PROVIDES
783 kJ, 187 kcal, 2 g protein, 11 g fat (7 g saturated fat), 19 g carbohydrate (17 g sugars), 2 g fibre, 24 mg sodium

desserts

# Waffles with syrupy strawberries

PREPARATION 10 minutes

COOKING 5 minutes

SERVES 4

## Shopping tip

Waffles come in different forms, from chunky Belgian-style to the smaller 'toaster' waffles. You'll find them in the supermarket bakery aisle or freezer section.

EACH SERVING PROVIDES
1641 kJ, 392 kcal, 10 g protein, 17 g fat (8 g saturated fat), 48 g carbohydrate (18 g sugars), 3 g fibre, 730 mg sodium

**250 g (8 oz) strawberries**

**¼ cup (60 ml) orange juice (freshly squeezed if possible)**

**2 tablespoons icing (confectioners') sugar**

**8 ready-made waffles**

**4 scoops vanilla ice cream**

1   Wash the strawberries and pat dry with paper towels. Remove the green tops, then cut the strawberries in half, or into quarters if large. Place in a shallow bowl.

2   Drizzle the orange juice over the strawberries. Sprinkle with the icing sugar and stir gently to combine. Allow the strawberries to soak for 5 minutes, turning them occasionally.

3   Meanwhile, toast the waffles according to the packet instructions.

4   Divide the waffles among serving plates. Top with the strawberries and their syrup and serve with a scoop of ice cream.

## Variations

- Use chocolate-chip ice cream instead of vanilla ice cream.
- Substitute whipped cream for the ice cream.

# Cheat's tiramisu

PREPARATION 10 minutes

COOKING none

SERVES 4

## Quick tip

Make sure the coffee is cooled to room temperature before using. To do this quickly, prepare the coffee with half the boiling water, then use cold water to make up the quantity to 1 cup (250 ml). You can use a good instant coffee if you like.

EACH SERVING PROVIDES
1457 kJ, 348 kcal, 5 g protein, 27 g fat (19 g saturated fat), 22 g carbohydrate (17 g sugars), <1 g fibre, 111 mg sodium

If you can, use dark (also known as 'Dutch') cocoa powder here, for its intense chocolatey flavour. Regular unsweetened cocoa powder will do in a pinch — or use grated dark chocolate instead.

**1 cup (250 ml) strong black coffee**

**250 g (8 oz) mascarpone**

**2 tablespoons icing (confectioners') sugar**

**8 savoiardi (lady finger biscuits)**

**1½ teaspoons dark unsweetened cocoa powder**

1 Pour the coffee into a bowl. Place the mascarpone in a mixing bowl, sift the icing sugar over and mix well.

2 Dip a biscuit into the coffee, turn to coat, then allow the coffee to drain back into the bowl. Dip and drain the biscuit again to ensure the coffee has soaked through to the middle. Break the soaked biscuit in half, then lay the halves in the base of a ¾ cup (180 ml) serving glass or bowl. Repeat with more biscuits and another three glasses.

3 Divide half the mascarpone mixture over the biscuits. Repeat with the remaining biscuits to make another layer in each glass. Top with a final layer of mascarpone.

4 Sift the cocoa powder over the top, through a small sieve. Serve immediately, or cover with plastic wrap and chill for up to 4 hours.

## Variation

Add a layer of raspberries after the first layer of mascarpone.

# Grilled pineapple

PREPARATION 10 minutes

COOKING 10 minutes

SERVES 4

## Variations

- You can use any type of liqueur or spirit instead of Grand Marnier — Malibu or rum are particularly good with pineapple.
- If you would rather not use alcohol, substitute a squeeze of lime juice instead.

EACH SERVING PROVIDES
689 kJ, 165 kcal, 2 g protein, 7 g fat (5 g saturated fat), 22 g carbohydrate (22 g sugars), 3 g fibre, 20 mg sodium

1 whole pineapple

2 teaspoons Grand Marnier or other orange-flavoured liqueur

2 tablespoons soft brown sugar

¼ cup (25 g) shredded coconut

4 scoops vanilla ice cream or reduced-fat vanilla yogurt

1   Preheat the grill (broiler) to high; line a large baking tray with foil. Cut the top and bottom from the pineapple, then cut off all the skin. Cut the pineapple crosswise into eight slices. Use a small biscuit or cookie cutter to cut the centre core from the each slice.

2   Arrange the pineapple on the baking tray. Drizzle with the liqueur, then sprinkle with the sugar. Grill (broil) for 7 minutes, or until the sugar has caramelised and is golden.

3   Meanwhile, place the coconut in a dry frying pan and stir over medium heat for 2 minutes, or until lightly toasted. Transfer to a plate to cool slightly.

4   Divide the pineapple pieces among serving plates and sprinkle with the coconut. Top each plate with a scoop of ice cream or yogurt and serve immediately.

# Tangy caramel bananas

1 small lime
50 g (1¾ oz) butter
½ cup (100 g) soft brown sugar
½ cup (125 ml) pouring (light) cream
4 small bananas

PREPARATION 10 minutes

COOKING 5 minutes

SERVES 4

1　Finely grate the zest of the lime, then squeeze the juice. Melt the butter in a large frying pan over medium heat. Add the sugar, lime zest and lime juice and stir until the sugar has dissolved.

2　Pour in the cream and stir until evenly combined. Cook over medium–low heat for 2 minutes, or until thickened slightly.

3　Peel the bananas and cut them diagonally into thick slices. Add the slices to the pan and gently turn to coat in the sauce. Allow to cool slightly before serving.

**Serving suggestion**
Sprinkle with chopped roasted, unsalted peanuts and serve with a scoop of vanilla ice cream.

## Variation

Fresh pineapple would be delicious instead of — or even as well as! — the bananas.

EACH SERVING PROVIDES
1343 kJ, 321 kcal, 2 g protein, 17 g fat
(11 g saturated fat), 42 g carbohydrate
(38 g sugars), 2 g fibre, 106 mg sodium

desserts

# Basics

These quick and easy recipes are a fabulous addition to your repertoire. Dip into this section whenever you're lost for inspiration or looking for a simple way to add flair to all manner of meals.

## Vinaigrette

**MAKES** about ⅓ cup (80 ml)     **PREPARATION** 5 minutes

**1 teaspoon dijon mustard**
**1 tablespoon vinegar**
**¼ cup (60 ml) olive oil**

Using a small whisk or a fork, whisk together the ingredients until evenly combined; alternatively, combine the ingredients in a small screw-top jar, seal tightly and shake well. Season to taste. Store in the fridge for up to 3 days. The oil may thicken or solidify when chilled, so return to room temperature before using.

**VARIATIONS**
• Use different types of vinegar — try balsamic, apple cider, herb-infused, raspberry, malt or red or white wine vinegar.
• Instead of vinegar use lemon, lime or orange juice.
• Use different types of oil, such as walnut, peanut or macadamia, or different grades of olive oil, from a peppery extra virgin to a milder type.
• Use wholegrain instead of dijon mustard.
• Add honey, some chopped fresh herbs or ground spices.

**COOK'S TIP** Always dress a leafy salad at the last minute, so the dressing doesn't make the leaves limp and soggy.

## Mayonnaise

**MAKES** 1⅓ cups (340 g)     **PREPARATION** 5 minutes

**2 egg yolks**
**1 teaspoon dijon mustard**
**1 tablespoon lemon juice**
**300 ml (10 fl oz/about 1¼ cups) light olive oil**
**ground white pepper, to taste**

1 Process the egg yolks, mustard and lemon juice in a food processor for 1 minute, or until combined and creamy.

2 With the motor running, add the oil, just a few drops at a time at first. As the mixture starts to thicken, add the oil in a thin stream — when all the oil has been added the mayonnaise should be thick and creamy. Season with salt and white pepper. Store in an airtight container in the fridge for up to 1 week.

**SERVING SUGGESTION** Use as a condiment, a spread on sandwiches, or as a salad dressing (thinned with a little more lemon juice and some water).

**VARIATIONS**
• **Aïoli** replace the mustard with 2 crushed garlic cloves.
• **Wasabi mayo** stir 2 teaspoons lime or lemon juice and 1–2 teaspoons wasabi into the finished mayonnaise.
• **Tartare sauce** stir in 2 chopped gherkins (pickles), 2 tablespoons finely chopped fresh parsley, 2 teaspoons chopped capers and 2 teaspoons finely grated lemon zest.

# Marvellous marinades

Marinades infuse flavour into meat, and also tenderise it. Place the meat or chicken in a shallow ceramic or glass dish (metal dishes can react with acidic ingredients and give an unpleasant taste). Drizzle with the marinade, cover with plastic wrap and refrigerate for as long as time allows. Ideally, marinate your meat or chicken for at least 1 hour, or up to 24 hours — but when you're pushed for time, marinating meat for even 10 minutes will impart some flavour.

When you're ready to cook, remove the meat from the marinade and let the excess liquid drain away. It's important to then pat the meat dry with paper towels — if the meat is too wet it will stew rather than sear when you begin to cook it.

These simple marinades take only a few minutes to prepare and will marinate about 500 g (1 lb) meat.

## Lemon, herb & garlic

Combine 2 tablespoons lemon juice, ½ cup (125 ml) olive oil, 2 crushed garlic cloves, 2 teaspoons each fresh thyme and chopped fresh rosemary. Cut slashes into boneless, skinless chicken breasts and pour the marinade over.

## Honey, soy & sesame

This marinade is delicious with chicken or beef. Combine ½ cup (125 ml) soy sauce, 2 tablespoons peanut oil, 2 tablespoons honey and 1 teaspoon sesame oil.

## Red wine & mustard

This marinade is perfect for steak. Whisk together ½ cup (125 ml) red wine, 2 tablespoons olive oil and 2 teaspoons wholegrain mustard.

COOK'S TIP If you want to use the marinade as a sauce, always bring it to a boil first and allow it to cook for several minutes to kill any bacteria from the raw meat.

## Lemon pepper

MAKES about 2 tablespoons   PREPARATION 10 minutes
COOKING 5 minutes

**2 large lemons**
**2 tablespoons black peppercorns**
**2 teaspoons coarse sea salt**

1 Preheat the oven to 150°C (300°F/Gas 2). Use a zester to cut fine shreds of lemon zest from the lemons. Spread the zest on a baking tray and bake for 5 minutes, or until dry but not coloured. Cool.

2 Use a mortar and pestle or small spice grinder to crush the lemon zest, peppercorns and salt together until evenly ground and combined. Store in an airtight container in a cool, dark place for up to 2 months. Sprinkle on meat, chicken or fish before cooking.

VARIATION For the Salt & Pepper Calamari recipe on page 183, coarsely grind together 1 tablespoon Sichuan peppercorns, 2 teaspoons sea salt, ½ teaspoon dried red chilli flakes and ¼ teaspoon black peppercorns. Store in an airtight container in a cool, dark place for up to 2 months.

## Moroccan spice mix

MAKES ½ cup (50 g)   PREPARATION 5 minutes

**¼ cup (40 g) mild paprika**
**1½ tablespoons ground coriander**
**1 tablespoon ground cinnamon**
**1½ teaspoons chilli powder**
**1 tablespoon ground allspice**

Combine all the spices in a screw-top jar. Store in a cool, dark place for up to 1 year.

COOK'S TIP This simple version is quite mild — for extra heat, add some extra chilli powder to the mix, or during cooking.

## Cajun spice mix

MAKES ½ cup   PREPARATION 5 minutes

**2 tablespoons ground sweet paprika**
**1½ tablespoons ground cumin**
**1 tablespoon ground fennel**
**1 tablespoon onion powder**
**1 teaspoon cayenne pepper**

Combine all the spices with a good pinch of salt in a screw-top jar. Store in a cool, dark place for up to 1 year. Dust over fish or chicken before pan-frying or barbecuing.

Homemade mayonnaise takes just minutes to make. It keeps for a week and you can jazz it up in so many ways.

## Red curry paste

MAKES about ¾ cup (185 g)  PREPARATION 10 minutes

½ bunch (45 g/1½ oz) coriander (cilantro),
  with the roots attached
8 long red chillies
1 lemongrass stem, white part only
2 cloves garlic
3 cm (1¼ inch) knob of fresh ginger

1 Wash the coriander roots to remove any grit, then roughly chop the stems, roots and leaves. Cut the chillies in half lengthwise, discard the seeds and chop the flesh. Slice the lemongrass and roughly chop the garlic and ginger.

2 Process all the ingredients in a food processor until finely chopped. With the motor running, add ¼ cup (60 ml) peanut oil in a thin stream to make a paste. Season to taste. Store in an airtight container in the fridge for up to 1 week.

VARIATION To make a green curry paste, replace the red chillies with green chillies.

COOK'S TIP Authentic optional additions include shrimp paste or fish sauce, lime juice and zest, makrut (kaffir lime) leaves, ground cumin and coriander seeds, fresh ground galangal and ground peppercorns.

## Harissa

MAKES ⅓ cup (90 g)  PREPARATION 10 minutes

4 long red chillies
2 cloves garlic
1 teaspoon ground cumin
1 teaspoon ground coriander

1 Cut the chillies in half lengthwise, discard the seeds and roughly chop the flesh. Crush the garlic.

2 Using a mortar and pestle or small food processor, pound the chilli, garlic and spices with 1 tablespoon olive oil and 1 teaspoon salt to form a smooth paste. Store in an airtight container in the fridge for up to 1 week.

SERVING SUGGESTION Use as a spicy addition to soups and stews, as a condiment with meat, chicken or fish, or spread onto meat, chicken or fish before cooking.

## Fresh Mexican salsa

MAKES 2 cups (400 g)  PREPARATION 10 minutes

2 large ripe tomatoes
½ small red onion
3 tablespoons coriander (cilantro) leaves
1 tablespoon lime juice
1 teaspoon finely chopped chilli (optional)

1 Cut the tomatoes in half, scoop out the seeds and dice the flesh. Finely dice the onion, and chop the coriander.

2 Combine the tomatoes, onion and coriander in a bowl with the lime juice and chilli, if using. Season to taste. Store, covered, in the fridge for up to 2 hours.

SERVING SUGGESTION Use in tacos or burritos, or on nachos. Serve with corn chips as a dip, or with any grilled (broiled) or barbecued meat, chicken or fish.

## Pesto

MAKES about 1 cup (250 g)  PREPARATION 10 minutes
COOKING 4 minutes

¼ cup (40 g) pine nuts
2 cups (100 g) basil leaves
2 cloves garlic, chopped
¼ cup (35 g) finely grated parmesan
½ cup (125 ml) extra virgin olive oil

1 Preheat the oven to 180°C (350°F/Gas 4). Spread the pine nuts on a baking tray and bake for 4 minutes, or until lightly golden. Transfer to a plate to cool.

2 Meanwhile, wash and dry the basil leaves. Place in a food processor with the pine nuts, garlic and parmesan and process until finely chopped.

3 With the motor running, add the oil in a thin stream, until the mixture is evenly combined and emulsified. Season to taste. Store in an airtight container in the fridge for up to 3 days. (To help preserve the colour, drizzle a thin layer of oil over the surface of the pesto before storing it.)

SERVING SUGGESTION Use as a pasta sauce, as a dip or spread, or as a condiment with meat, fish or chicken.

Hey presto — you only need five ingredients and ten minutes to whip up a batch of fresh pesto!

## Barbecue sauce

MAKES 1 cup (250 ml)   PREPARATION 5 minutes
COOKING 3 minutes

1 cup (250 ml) tomato passata (puréed tomatoes)
1 tablespoon soft brown sugar
3 teaspoons worcestershire sauce
2 teaspoons malt vinegar
¼ teaspoon ground allspice

Combine all the ingredients in a small saucepan; stir over low heat until the ingredients are evenly combined and the sugar has dissolved. Store in an airtight container in the fridge for up to 5 days.

COOK'S TIP Use as a condiment with barbecued meat, or use to brush over chicken drumsticks before roasting.

## Satay sauce

MAKES 1½ cups (375 ml)   PREPARATION 5 minutes
COOKING 3 minutes

½ cup (140 g) peanut butter
1 cup (250 ml) coconut milk
1½ tablespoons sweet chilli sauce (or more, to taste)
2 teaspoons soy sauce
2 teaspoons lime juice

Combine all the ingredients in a small saucepan; stir over medium heat until smooth and heated through. Store in an airtight container in the fridge for up to 3 days.

SERVING SUGGESTION Use as a dipping sauce for vegetable crudités, or as a sauce for chicken or beef skewers.

## Ponzu sauce

MAKES about ⅔ cup (150 ml)   PREPARATION 10 minutes
COOKING 2 minutes

⅓ cup (80 ml) soy sauce
⅓ cup (80 ml) lemon juice
1 teaspoon rice vinegar
1 teaspoon grated fresh ginger
3 teaspoons caster (superfine) sugar

1 Combine all the ingredients in a small saucepan; stir over low heat until the sugar has dissolved.

2 Strain through a fine sieve and cool. Store in an airtight container in the fridge for up to 3 days. Use as a dipping sauce in Japanese recipes, or as a dressing or marinade.

SHORTCUT INGREDIENT Use grated ginger from a jar.

## Black olive tapenade

MAKES ¾ cup (185 g)   PREPARATION 10 minutes

1 cup (150 g) pitted kalamata olives
2 anchovy fillets (canned anchovies)
2 teaspoons capers
1 small clove garlic, crushed
1 tablespoon olive oil

Combine all the ingredients in a small food processor and process until almost smooth. Store in an airtight container in the fridge for up to 1 week. Use as a dip or spread, or as a condiment.

VARIATION To make a green olive tapenade, use pitted green olives instead of kalamata olives.

## Hummus

MAKES about 1½ cups (330 g)   PREPARATION 10 minutes

**420 g (15 oz) can chickpeas**
**1 clove garlic, chopped**
**2 tablespoons tahini**
**2 tablespoons lemon juice**
**½ teaspoon ground cumin**

1 Drain the chickpeas into a sieve and rinse under cold running water. Drain well and place in a food processor with the remaining ingredients. Process until smooth.

2 Add 2 tablespoons olive oil and 1 tablespoon water. Process again until smooth and light, then season to taste. Store in an airtight container in the fridge for up to 3 days.

SERVING SUGGESTION Use as a dip or spread.

## Tabouleh

SERVES 4–6   PREPARATION 10 minutes

**⅓ cup (60 g) burghul (bulgur)**
**1 bunch (150 g/5 oz) flat-leaf parsley**
**2 tomatoes**
**2 spring onions (scallions)**
**2 tablespoons lemon juice**

1 Place the burghul in a heatproof bowl and add ⅓ cup (80 ml) boiling water. Stand for 10 minutes.

2 Meanwhile, pick all the parsley leaves from the stems. Roughly chop the parsley, dice the tomatoes and slice the spring onions. Combine in a bowl with the burghul, lemon juice and 1 tablespoon olive oil, then season to taste. Store, covered, in the fridge for up to 2 days.

SERVING SUGGESTION Use as a side salad, on sandwiches and in wraps.

## Tzatziki

MAKES about 1½ cups (375 g)   PREPARATION 10 minutes

**1 Lebanese or other small cucumber**
**1 spring onion (scallion)**
**1 clove garlic**
**1 cup (250 g) Greek-style yogurt**
**1 teaspoon finely chopped fresh dill**

1 Coarsely grate the cucumber. Take handfuls of the cucumber and squeeze out the excess liquid over a bowl; discard the liquid.

2 Finely slice the spring onion and place in a bowl. Crush the garlic into the bowl and add the cucumber, yogurt and dill. Mix well and season to taste. Store in an airtight container in the fridge for up to 1 week.

SERVING SUGGESTION Use as a dip, or as an accompaniment to fish or chicken.

## Sponge cake

**MAKES** 1 double sponge   **PREPARATION** 10 minutes
**COOKING** 15 minutes

4 eggs
²⁄₃ cup (150 g) caster (superfine) sugar
1 teaspoon vanilla extract
1 cup (150 g) self-raising flour

1 Preheat the oven to 190°C (375°F/Gas 5). Lightly grease two 20 cm (8 inch) round cake tins and line the bases with baking (parchment) paper.

2 Meanwhile, using electric beaters, beat the eggs in a large bowl for 5 minutes, or until thick and pale. Add the sugar gradually, beating well after each addition. Beat in the vanilla.

3 Sift the flour over the egg mixture and, using a large metal spoon, fold it in until combined, taking care not to lose too much volume. Divide the batter evenly between the cake tins.

4 Bake for 15 minutes, or until the cakes spring back when lightly touched in the centre. Cool in the tins for 5 minutes, then turn out onto a wire rack to cool completely. Store in an airtight container in the fridge for up to 1 week.

**SERVING SUGGESTION** Sandwich together with whipped cream, cut up to make into lamingtons, or cut into smaller pieces and use in a trifle (see our Peach Trifle on page 295).

Nutritious and delicious, quick and easy tabouleh adds a dash of Middle Eastern magic to many different meals.

## Custard

**MAKES** about 1½ cups (375 ml)   **PREPARATION** 5 minutes
**COOKING** 8 minutes

1¼ cups (310 ml) milk
3 egg yolks
¼ cup (55 g) caster (superfine) sugar
3 teaspoons cornflour (cornstarch)
1 teaspoon vanilla extract

1 Heat the milk in a saucepan until it just boils. Meanwhile, use a wire whisk to beat the yolks, sugar and cornflour in a bowl until light and creamy.

2 Gradually pour the hot milk onto the egg mixture, stirring constantly. Transfer the mixture to a clean saucepan and stir over low heat for 5 minutes, or until thickened enough to coat the back of a spoon. Stir in the vanilla.

3 Store, covered, in the fridge for up to 2 days.

**SERVING SUGGESTION** Use warm over pies and puddings, or allow to cool and use in a trifle, such as our Peach Trifle on page 295.

## Easy crepes

**MAKES** 8 crepes   **PREPARATION** 5 minutes
**COOKING** about 15 minutes

²⁄₃ cup (100 g) plain (all-purpose) flour
2 eggs
330 ml (11 fl oz/about 1¹⁄₃ cups) milk

1 Sift the flour into a bowl and make a well in the centre. Whisk the eggs and milk together, then gradually add to the flour, whisking gently until smooth.

2 Lightly oil a 20 cm (8 inch) crepe pan or non-stick frying pan. Pour ¼ cup (60 ml) of batter into the pan, swirling to coat the base. Cook over medium heat for 1 minute on each side, or until lightly golden. Repeat to make eight crepes.

3 Use straight away, or allow the crepes to cool and stack them, placing a sheet of baking (parchment) paper between each crepe. Wrap the stack in plastic, then seal tightly in a zip-lock bag (with all the air expelled) and freeze for up to 2 months. Use in sweet or savoury crepe recipes.

**COOK'S TIP** Don't beat the batter vigorously, or the crepes will be tough.

# Index

**PROJECT EDITOR** Katri Hilden
**WRITER** Tracy Rutherford
**SENIOR DESIGNER** Donna Heldon
**DESIGNER** Kylie Mulquin
**RECIPES** Jo Anne Calabria, Tracy Rutherford, Kerrie Sun
and Brigid Treloar
**PHOTOGRAPHER** Ian Hofstetter
**STYLIST** Trish Heagerty
**FOOD PREPARATION** Grace Campbell and Wendy Quisumbing
**NUTRITIONAL ANALYSIS** Toni Gumley
**PROOFREADER** Susan McCreery
**INDEXER** Diane Harriman
**SENIOR PRODUCTION CONTROLLER** Monique Tesoriero
**EDITORIAL PROJECT MANAGER GENERAL BOOKS** Deborah Nixon
**READER'S DIGEST GENERAL BOOKS**
**EDITORIAL DIRECTOR** Elaine Russell
**MANAGING EDITOR** Rosemary McDonald
**ART DIRECTOR** Carole Orbell

Library of Congress Cataloging-in-Publication Data available upon
request

ISBN 978-1-60652-326-1

We are committed to both the quality of our products and the
service we provide to our customers. We value your comments, so
please feel free to contact us.

The Reader's Digest Association, Inc.
Adult Trade Publishing
44 S. Broadway
White Plains, NY 10601

Prepress by Sinnott Bros, Sydney
Printed and bound by Leo Paper Products, China

1 3 5 7 9 10 8 6 4 2

## Notes to our Readers

### Weights and measures

Ingredients are generally listed by their weight or volume with cup
measurements given for convenience, unless the conversion is
imperfect, whereby the ingredients are listed by weight or volume
only. Sometimes conversions within a recipe are not exact but are
the closest conversion that is a suitable measurement for each
system. Use either the metric or the imperial measurements; do
not mix the two systems.

### Can sizes

Can sizes vary among countries and manufacturers; if the stated
size is unavailable, use the nearest equivalent. Here are
approximate metric and imperial measurements for common can
sizes.
225 g = 8 oz; 300 g = 10 oz; 350 g = 12 oz;
400/410 g = 14 oz = 398 ml/410 ml;
800 g = 28 oz = 796 ml

### Nutritional analysis

Serving suggestions, garnishes and optional ingredients are not
included in the nutritional analysis. Oil has not been included in
the five-ingredient count, in or the nutritional analysis. Most
recipes use about 1 tablespoon of oil for frying or serving, which
equates to 1 teaspoon per serving for recipes that serve 4. A
teaspoon of oil will add about 168 kJ (40 kcaJ) and 4.5 g fat (0.5 g
saturated fat) to a serving.

### Alternative terms and substitutes

**CAPSICUM** sweet pepper, bell pepper
**CHINESE FIVE SPICE** five spice powder
**CORIANDER** cilantro
**CORN COB** mealie/miele
**CREAM, POURING** (light) table cream
**EGGPLANT** aubergine, brinjal
**ENGLISH SPINACH** baby spinach
**FISH SUBSTITUTES** for firm white-fleshed fish use
cod, hake or kabeljou
**FRESH SHIITAKE MUSHROOMS** rehydrated dried
shiitake mushrooms
**HOKKIEN NOODLES** 2-minute or fast-cooking noodles
**KECAP MANIS** sweet soy sauce
**LEBANESE CUCUMBER** Mediterranean cucumber,
short cucumber
**OREGANO** oreganum
**PAPAYA** pawpaw
**PASSIONFRUIT** granadilla
**SWISS BROWN MUSHROOMS** brown mushrooms
**VANILLA EXTRACT** vanilla essence
**VIETNAMESE MINT** mint or cilantro and mint
**WITLOT** witloof, Belgian endive
**ZUCCHINI** baby marrow, courgette

**FRONT COVER UPPER IMAGES, LEFT TO RIGHT:**
Lamb & chickpeas with chargrilled eggplant, page 153
Chicken & leek sauté, page 125
Pasta with chicken meatballs, page 105
Chicken pizzas, page 126
**FRONT COVER LOWER IMAGE:** Rice noodle papaya salad, page 90
**BACK COVER IMAGES, LEFT TO RIGHT:**
Pumpkin soup, page 29
Quick apple crumble, page 296
Beetroot, rocket & goat's cheese salad, page 86
Thai beef salad, page 85